Beating the fund managers

Tony Pow

Why you invest

You need to learn about investing sooner or later in your life. You need to take some calculated risks.

Compare the returns of the following assets: cash, CDs, treasury bills, bonds, real estate and stocks. We start with the risk-free investments and end with the riskiest. It turns out that the average returns are in the opposite order. Cash and CDs are not risk-free as inflation eats our profits. For example, the real return is negative for the 2% return in a CD and a 3% inflation rate. In addition you have to pay taxes for the 'returns'. Our capitalist system punishes us for not taking risk.

There are two kinds of risk: blind risk and calculated risk. If you buy a stock due to a recommendation from a commentator on TV or a tip, most likely you are taking a blind risk. It would be the same in buying a house without thoroughly evaluating the house and its neighborhood. When you buy stocks with a proven strategy (i.e. when/what stocks to buy and when/what stocks to sell), you are taking a calculated risk. In the long run, stocks with calculated and educated risks are profitable.

Be a turtle investor by investing in value stocks and holding for longer time periods (a year or more). "Buy and Monitor" is better an approach than "Buy and Hold" as some could lose all the stock values such as in the failure of Enron.

For experienced investors, shorting, short-term trading and covered calls would make you good profits. Simple market timing would reduce your losses during market down turns. If you buy a market ETF and use my simple market timing, you should have beaten the market by a wide margin from 2000 to 2019. With so many frauds and poor management, do not trust anyone with your investing. Do not buy investing instruments that are highly marketed such as annuity and term insurance.

If you are a handy man and do not mind to satisfy the constant requests of your tenants, buy real estate in growing areas could be very profitable in the long run. Take advantage of the tax laws such as investing in a 401K especially the part that is matched by your company and/or a Roth IRA.

Why you want to read this book

It should improve your financial health substantially.

- This book has more than 120 pages (6*9) and is about double the size of its competitors with similar price range.

- A best seller was written by a young writer whose main income was from his books and none from his investing. Most of my income is from investing.

- Many popular books claiming the authors making millions. However, usually their techniques are hard to follow. Many admitted they had been bankrupted many times. My techniques minimize risking our money. Paper test your technique first. I prefer to be a 'turtle investor'.

- There are many popular books combining technical and some fundamentals. They worked very well at one time and folks making millions following the advice. However, look at their recent performances of the last five years.

- One book describes ROE as the only theme (with the story of the life of the author to fill up the book). This book includes many basic metrics such as P/E.

My motivation to write this book

I would like to share my experiences, both good and bad. I use simple-to-follow techniques using the free (or low-cost) resources available to us.

My article

It could be the top-performed article in Seeking Alpha, an investing site, for recommending 10 or more stocks in a year from its published date. So far, no one challenges me. I will not write another similar article as I cannot top this one. However, the reasons why I selected these stocks are included in my books.

https://seekingalpha.com/article/2492255-a-tale-of-2-portfolios

Contents

Institutional investors

Institutional investors include banks, hedge funds, insurance companies and mutual funds. They are important as they move the market, not the retail investors.

You want to follow them closely. When they buy specific stocks, buy the same stocks and vice versa. It is better to be one step before their actions. Due to their large holdings, usually it takes more than a week for them to finish the trade. Basically this is how day traders make money by jumping into their wagons. When you see a sudden surge in volume of a specific stock, there is a good chance the institutional investors are trading.

Several sites including GuruFocus.com keep track of the stocks they are holding and their current trades. Finviz.com has similar information. IBD gives a higher rating to the stocks that are held by institutional investors.

Normally the stocks owned by the institutional investors have larger market caps (over 1 billion) and most have stock prices over $10.

Once a while, their trades are not rational. When you act against them, you need a good reason and be patient.

I took advantages of them using Apple for illustration:

- Recommended in my book Scoring Stocks to buy Apple in June, 2013 (the publish date) while most of the institutional investors were dumping Apple. Apple scored very high in my book then.
- Recommended to sell Apple in my blog in Feb., 2015 when Apple was $132. The profit is about $60 per share from the recommended dates.
- Took advantage of the correction making 12% in 2015 for holding Apple in about 2 months.

Taking advantages of fund managers

Fund managers have the best resources in investing. However, we can beat the fund managers by taking advantages of their restrictions and limitations as described below:

- Their hefty fees. It is about 1.5%. Most charge more. They have hidden fees such as using their in-house brokers. I am paying $5 per trade and even less when using selected ETFs. The ETFs have comparatively low maintenance cost than the average cost of mutual funds.
- Most mutual fund managers have to sell some of their stocks when their clients sell the mutual funds. When there is blood in the street, it could be the best time to buy.
- Most mutual fund managers cannot time the market. We, the retail investors, can.
- Most mutual fund managers cannot trade stocks less than 1 billion and/or the stock price less than $5. We can.
- The high volumes of their trades are usually seen by the day traders who take advantage of it by riding the wagon.

#Filler: Miss Mia

In my first job just after the Vietnam War, every one tried to date my beautiful office mate Mia except me. If we married, then her name would be Mia Pow. She would be very popular, or very unpopular without showing her beautiful face. In any case, when she becomes a mother, she will be Mamma Mia.

BTW. I was the "comfort man" due to the gender gap during the Vietnam War.

Hedge fund 101

LTCM (a hedge fund named Long Term Capital Management), with two Nobel-prize winners, an excellent support team and the best technologies then, ran their hedge funds into the ground. Many hedge funds are closed due to fraud, and/or poor performance.

The primary purpose is supposed to 'hedge' your investments from market plunges / dips. Since 2008, the government has printed so much money, and it make the market recover and make the hedges (shorts, derivatives, etc.) unnecessary. In reality, most hedge funds today do not hedge.

Hedge funds get tons of press coverage as a Holy Grail type of investing. The media needs the advertising from this $2.5 trillion industry. It is similar to mutual funds but they take more risk for supposedly better returns. Most require higher minimum investments and more restrictions such as requiring longer periods before you can withdraw your money.

It could be the worst deal to most of their customers: 2% average up front and 20% average on your profit. It is more acceptable to me if the 20% is on profit over the S&P 500 return. Why should I pay you 20% on my 10% profit when the market rises by 15%? In this case, my fund loses 5% relative to the market.

Well, if they consistently make a lot of money for you, maybe it is not too much to object to. However, most risk your money by betting big recklessly. When they win, they get 20% of your profit and they use you for advertising to lure in other suckers. When they lose *your* money, they do not lose a penny. It encourages them to take big risks. I do not know any hedge fund (HF) manager who pays you back for your losses.

An average mutual fund charges about 1.5% in management fees. An average hedge fund charges 2% so that would cover the expenses to run their office, market the products and for research expenses. The real compensation of an average hedge fund depends on the average 20% of the profit.

You would have better return by investing in a no-load index fund, or a diversified ETF than an average hedge fund. To calculate the average hedge fund performance, you need to include the many hedge funds that are out of business. To illustrate my pint, check out the performance of SPY in the last five years and that of the average hedge fund. However, SPY and similar ETFs are risky due to the heavy weighing on winners such as FAANGs.

After a hedge fund has failed, most fund managers just open another hedge fund (if they do not go to jail first due to fraud) and give you all the excuse for losing your hard-earned money. Some lose their reputation but you need to check them out well before you hire another one.

In 2011, the hedge fund industry did not beat the S&P 500 index fund after their fees. I bet the hedge fund industry will not beat the market after 2011.

Some hedge fund managers learn modern portfolio theories from Ivy League universities and apply them in the hedge funds. Often their theories are based on wrong testing procedures, or they cannot be sustained in real life.

Many invest in new companies and small companies where they would have big profit swings. They need to learn the business of the company in which they plan to buy the stocks, interview the owners, read between the lines, and double check whether the owners are telling the truth by talking to their competitors, vendors and customers. It explains the high cost for their research. We just need to look at the transactions of the insiders and/or use a low-cost subscription to find similar type of research. There is no need to travel to visit the company unless you want to.

Some use their specialties in certain sectors and that's fine. If they use derivatives, be careful and that's what resulted in our 2007 financial crisis. Derivatives could reduce the risk of the portfolio if they are properly used. If you still want to invest in them, ask for their methods and their historical performance. Very few hedge funds are good. When you find a good hedge fund, most likely it has been closed to new investors or its fees are outrageous.

The owner of a famous baseball franchise lost big money from a hedge fund that concentrated in the oil sector. Almost every ETF in this sector made good money that year, but he still stayed with the hedge fund and had similar miserable returns the following year. I did not blame him for his first mistake, but on his sticking with the same hedge fund after a losing year. It could be that the hedge fund gave him a hard time when he wanted to take his money out or he could be busy in his baseball franchise.

One hedge fund has a performance of 25% every year over a long period of time. The SEC, takes notes and then investigates whether they were using insiders' information. There are very few hedge funds with consistent performance beating the market after their hefty fees. If you find some, stay with them forever. One hedge fund was rated as the top fund and the next year it was out of business due to poor performance. Hedge fund managers chase after short-term returns as the outflow will be serious if they do not perform well. When they were successful recently, they had a hard time to perform with an excessive inflow of money. Both cost underperformance in the fund.

In 1980, this industry started with really capable fund managers and made good money for their clients. After that, every analyst wanted to open a hedge fund and most did not even beat the market after their fees. Alternatively, just buy the ETF SPY and relax, instead of waiting for the hedge fund to wipe out your savings. You need to know that this industry is not properly regulated.

Do not believe in any articles / ads praising how great the hedge funds are without knowing their credibility and any hidden agendas. The hedge fund indexes usually ignore the survivor bias of the bankrupted hedge funds and the early exits of many hedge funds.

Since the hedge funds very seldom keep the stocks more than a year, their capital gains would be short-term and hence would be taxed at a higher rate than the long-term capital gains. In addition, most funds have a 1-3 year lock-up period and only allow withdrawals on the first day of each fiscal quarter.

Introduction

This book is targeted to beginner investors and/or couch potatoes who do not want to spend a lot of time in managing their investments. With the limitations / restrictions of fund managers, we can beat them.

This book helps someone looking for simple but profitable strategies in investing. It only takes about half an hour a month to monitor the market and decide what stocks to buy and sell.

This book uses the advanced strategies described in my other books but in very simplified instructions. The trick is to make them easy to use from the research information available to us free of charge.

This book consists of 4 sections: Simple Techniques, Finding Stocks, Strategies and Advanced Topics.

I start with market timing. You should not buy any stocks when the market is plunging. Actually you should sell most of the stocks you own when the market is plunging. For those who can take more risk, buy contra ETFs betting the market is plunging. I have a simple way to spot market plunges. It is based on charts. However, you can obtain similar info without creating charts and there is nothing to subscribe and buy. Although past performances are not guarantee for the future, following the techniques that work for the last two crashes (as of 6/2017) is better than not using any technique.

The chart tells us when to reenter the market for the best opportunity to make money. I did in 2003 and 2009.

Corrections provide opportunities to buy stocks. However, you have to prepare for the next correction by accumulating cash in advance and preparing a list of stocks you want to buy and at what prices. If you do not have such a list, just buy one or more ETFs.

For starters, just trade ETFs and you can skip the latter chapters in evaluating stocks.

In the simplest terms, I discussed how to evaluate stocks fundamentally and technically. Use the research available in the free sites such as Finviz.com. Instead of spending hours in researching one stock, you can do the same in a few minutes as others have researched them for you.

Many chapters are derived from my book "Complete the Art of Investing". I take out the techniques that require time and extensive knowledge.

I am not a writer but a retail investor similar to most of you. I've been making a comfortable living via my investment ideas that I'm sharing in this book.

Retail investors have a lot of advantages over fund managers. However, I advise not to be a trader especially day traders for beginners. Statistically most amateur traders lose money as they cannot compete with experienced, disciplined traders. Even if you study several good books by great traders, most likely you will still lose money initially. No books can replace the actual trading experience.

For beginner investors

Both Fidelity and AAII (both require being a client or a member) have excellent articles for beginners. Alternatively, buy a book for beginners. To include all the basic terms and concepts, I have to double the size of this book which is already lengthy and bore most readers who already have the basic knowledge.

Click here for Morningstar classroom.
http://morningstar.com/cover/classroom.html

Click here for Fidelity basic in investing.
https://www.fidelity.com/investment-guidance/investing-basics

How this book is organized

Most graphs are in landscape orientation for both paperback and e-readers. Some graphs may not be displayed adequately on a small screen of an e-reader. E-readers may be available in the current version of Windows, so you can read e-books on the larger screen of your PC. For better orientation, just flip the e-readers 90 degrees.

A link is usually included for these screens. Copy it to your browser to display the graphs on your PC if desirable. Instructions on how to produce some graphs are provided as you should try them out. One example is how to produce a chart on detecting market crashes.

It is easier to display some tables in landscape mode, which can be selected in your e-reader. Select a table or a graph via your e-reader to display it to fit the screen.

The font size and page size of most e-book formats can be adjusted. The unknown, special character is the "smiling face" that the current Kindle does not convert correctly as of this writing.

There are clickable links to web articles. Most of them are from my own web sites and public web sites such as Wikipedia. Some public links may not be available in the future as they are not under my control.

Fidelity Video provides video clips to explain some basic terms and it may require Fidelity customers to sign on in order to view them. Check the trial offer from Fidelity. YouTube offers similar video lessons.

These links extend the usefulness of this book by making available specific topics that may not be interesting to every reader.

The current version provides most of the links the paperback readers can enter into your browser. Get the same information by entering a search in Wikipedia such as Dogs of Dow.

Investopedia is another source beside Wikipedia.
http://www.investopedia.com/

'Afterthoughts' includes my additional comments and comments from others. Readers can make comments in this book's website. There are fillers with tips and jokes to fill up the empty space of the printed book.

For convenience, this book uses SPY, an Exchange Traded Fund (ETF) simulating S&P 500, as the benchmark for the market.

Annualized returns (Return * 365 / (Days between)) are used where appropriate for more meaningful comparison. To illustrate, I have a 10% return in 6 months, a 10% in a year and a 10% in 2 years. It is more meaningful to use annualized returns of 20%, 10% and 5%

respectively for the 6-month return, the one-year return and the 2-year return in this example.

Usually I do not include the dividend, so you can add an estimated 1.5% to the annualized return. In addition, compound interest is not used for easier calculation, so the actual return could be even better.

About the author

I graduated from Cal. State University at San Jose in Industrial Engineering and University of Mass. in Amherst with a MS in Industrial Engineering. I have been an investor for over 30 years.

Dedication

To all retail investors and future retail investors including my grandchildren.

Acknowledgement

Thanks to: Seeking Alpha, Wikipedia and Investopedia for the many helpful links to enrich this book. Yahoo!Finance and Finviz.com for the tools and charts used in this book.

Important notices

© 2018-2022 Tony Pow. Email ID: pow_tony@yahoo.com.

Version	Paperback	eBooks
1.00	01/18	01/18
2.00	10/19	10/19
2.03	12/21	12/21

Book store managers can order the paper version of this book from Createspace.com.
https://tonyp4idea.blogspot.com/2020/12/book-managers.html
Book update.
https://ebmyth.blogspot.com/2020/12/updates-for-all-books.html

If you are reading my concise version (100 pages or less) and find it useful, you may want to check out "Complete the art of investing" which has over 850 pages (Kindle version).

Disclaimer

Section I: Simple techniques

Introduction

For starters, just trade ETFs such as SPY (an ETF simulating the market), and you can skip the rest of the book. It only takes a few minutes every month. When the market is not plunging, buy or keep SPY (or any ETF that stimulates the market); otherwise sell it. Do the opposite when the market is recovering.

If you have less than $50,000 to invest, just buy ETFs. Improve your investing skills by reading investment articles from this book and your broker's website. For example, Fidelity has a lot of information for investors.

Subscription to AAII is recommended. When your portfolio grows more than $50,000, invest on a subscription such as Value Line, GuruFocus, Zacks or IBD (more for momentum traders). Initially, use the information for paper trading on value stocks, which is usually available from brokers.

For the long term, knowledge is most important in your investing life and experience comes next. Retail investors have a lot of advantages over fund managers. However, I advise you NOT to be a trader. Hence, you should ignore the 'fabulous' trade systems that claim to be very profitable. Statistically most amateur traders lose money as they cannot compete with experienced, disciplined traders.

How to start

I recommend trading ETFs first and when the market is not risky. The very basic terms such as ETF are not fully explained here; try Investopedia for terms you need to know. Otherwise this book would be doubled in size and it would bore most readers. Investopedia, your broker's website (especially Fidelity) and AAII (requiring subscription) provide many excellent articles. Alternatively, buy a book for beginners. Here are some freebies:

Click here for Morningstar classroom.
http://morningstar.com/cover/classroom.html
Click here for Vanguard.
https://investor.vanguard.com/investing/investor-education
Click here for Investopedia's Tutorials.

http://www.investopedia.com/university/
Click here for Yahoo!
http://finance.yahoo.com/education/begin_investing
Click here for Fidelity basic in investing.
https://www.fidelity.com/investment-guidance/investing-basics

1   Simplest market timing

Why market timing

Before 2000, market timing was a waste of time. However after that, we have had two market plunges with the average loss of about 45%. It sounds harder to time the market than it actually is. We have a simple technique to detect market plunges and when to reenter the market. Our objective is reducing the loss to 25%.

Market timing depends on charts; the following describes how to use chart information without creating charts. Most charts will not identify the peaks and bottoms of the market as they depend on data (i.e. the stock prices). However, it would reduce further losses. It is simpler than it sounds. Just follow the procedure below.

The first part of this technique detects market plunges, and the second part advises you when to reenter the market. It applies to individual stocks too. It also works to detect the trend of a sector (entering an ETF for the specific sector instead of SPY) and a specific stock.

How to detect market plunges without charts (a.k.a. Death Cross)
1.   Bring up Finviz.com.

2.   Enter SPY (or any ETF that simulates the market) or RSP for equally weighed SPY.

3.   If SMA-200% is positive, it indicates that the market plunge has not been detected and you can skip the following steps.

4.   The market is plunging if SMA-50% is more negative than SMA-200%. To illustrate this condition, SMA-200% is -2% and SMA-50% is -5%.

5.   Sell most stocks starting with the riskiest ones first such as the ones with negative earnings, high P/Es and/or high Debt/Equity.

Obtain this info from Finviz.com by entering the symbol of the stock you own.

6. Conservative investors should sell only those overpriced stocks. Aggressive investors should sell all stocks. Extremely aggressive investors should sell all stocks, buy contra ETFs, and even short stocks. I do not recommend beginners to be aggressive.

When to return to the market (a.k.a. Golden Cross)

Use the above in a reversed sense to detect whether the market has been recovering. However, when the SMA-200% turns positive, I would start buying value stocks (low P/E but the 'E' has to be positive, and/or low Debt/Equity).

1. Bring up Finviz.com.
2. Enter SPY (or any ETF that simulates the market).
3. If SMA-200% is negative, the market is not recovering, and you can skip the following steps.
4. Sell all contra ETFs and close all shorts if you have any.
5. Market recovery is confirmed when SMA-50% is more positive than SMA-200%. To illustrate this condition, SMA-200% is 2% and SMA-50% is 5%. Commit a large percent of cash (or all cash for aggressive investors) to stocks. If you do not know what to buy, buy SPY or an ETF that simulates the market.

How often to check the market timing indicators
Do the above once a month. When the SPY price is closer to SMA actions percentage, perform the above once a week. The charts and data for market timing described in this book are based on SMA-350 (Simple Moving Average) that is more preferable than this simple procedure, but it requires some simple charting.

Nothing is perfect
If the market timing is perfect, there would be no poor folks. The major 'defects' are:
*   It does not detect the peak / bottom as it depends on past data. However, it would save you a lot during the crash.
*   It is hard to determine whether it is a correction or a crash.
*   From 2000 to 2010, there was only one false signal. The indicator tells you to exit and then tells you to reenter the market shortly. In most cases, you do not lose a lot. After 2010, we have more false signals.

2   Quick analysis of ETFs

Evaluate an ETF

ETFs are a basket of stocks according to the market, a specific sector, country or a specific theme.

Yahoo!Finance used to give the P/E of an ETF. Try to get it from ETFdb.com. Enter the symbol of the ETF such as XLU, and then select Valuation. If it is below 15 and above zero, it could be a value ETF. Also, if the current price is lower than its NAV, it is sold at a discount (or premium vice versa). Compare its YTD Return to SPY's.

Alternatively, get similar info from http://www.multpl.com/. In addition, this website provides the following metrics: Shiller P/E, Price/Sales, and Price/Book.

From Finviz.com, enter the ETF symbol. If SMA-20%, SMA-50% and SMA-200% are all positive, most likely the ETF is in an uptrend. To illustrate, SMA-200 is Simple Moving Average for the last 200 trading sessions (no trading on weekends and specific holidays). The percent is how much the stock price of the ETF is above the SMA. If the percent is negative, it means the stock price is below the SMA.

If your average holding period of your stocks is about 50 days, SMA-50% is more appropriate to you.

If RSI(14) > 65, it is probably oversold; if it is < 30, it is probably under-sold (indicating value).

In addition, ensure the ETF's average volume is high (I suggest more than 10,000 shares), the market cap is more than 300 M, and it has low fees. Most popular ETFs have these characteristics. Beginners should avoid leveraged ETFs.

How to determine if the sector has been recovered

It is easier to profit by following the uptrend of an ETF using the above info. It is hard to detect when the bottom of an ETF has been reached. If SMA-20%, SMA-50% and SMA-200% are all positive, most likely the ETF is in an uptrend or it has recovered. It does not always happen as predicted, so use stops to protect your investment.

An example

First, determine whether the market is risky. Most beginners should not invest in a risky market. Advanced investors can bet against the market or a specific sector by buying contra ETFs or puts.

Next, you want to limit the number of sector ETFs by selecting those that are either in an uptrend or hitting bottom (bottom is hard to predict). Personally I prefer sectors with long-term uptrends (indicated by articles found in many websites including cnnfn.com and Seeking Alpha.

For illustration purposes only for deteriorating market conditions, I would select the following ETFs: SPY (simulating the market based on large companies) and XLP (consumer staples). XLP should perform better than XLY (consumer discretionary) during a recession as those products are the necessities.

Technical indicators such as SMA-50 (Simple Moving Average for the last 50 sessions), SMA-200 and RSI(14) are obtained from Finviz.com and the rest are obtained from Yahoo!Finance.com. After you buy the ETF, use a stop loss to protect your investment. For example, biotech sector moved up for many months until it crashed in 2015. Change the stop loss value every month to protect your gains in this case.

As of 2/5/2016	SPY	XLP (staples)	XLY (discret.)
Price	190	50	71
NAV	192	50	73
• Technical			
SMA-50	-4%	0%	-7%
SMA-200	-6%	2%	-7%
RSI(14)	44	50	36
Other	Double bottom at $186		
• Fundamental			
P/E	17	20	19
Yield	2.1%	2.5%	1.5%
YTD return	-5%	0.5%	-5%
Net asset	174 B	9 B	10 B

Explanation

- The figures may not be identical among websites due to the dates they are using.
- XLY has the best discount among the 3 ETFs as most investors believe a recession is coming.
- XLP has less down trend among the 3 ETFs as expected.
- XLY is more undersold among the three as expected.
- Double bottom is a technical pattern that indicates the stock would surge upward.
- SPY has a better value according to its P/E.
- XLY's dividend is the least among the three as they have more tech companies in the ETF. They have to plow back the profits to research and development.
- XLP has the best YTD return among the three.
- As long as the asset is above 500 M (200 M for specialized ETFs), it is fine and all three pass this mark.

There are many metrics such as Debt/Equity not readily available from most websites. Many sites list the top holdings of a specific ETF. Just average the metrics of the top ten or so of its stock holdings.

#Filler: Illogical logic

If we do not test for the pandemic, we would have zero increase in this pandemic. Some silly folks buy this argument. What happens to the once-great country?

Filler: The problems of the U.S.

1. Our political system. We waste time arguing between the two parties. There is no long-term planning, as the other party could claim the credit. Same as corporations' CEOs who care about their yearly bonuses.
2. The politicians have to satisfy their voters. Today give them free cash by jacking up the printing press. And ignore the long-term consequences.
3. We have to protect our workers, our environment... Hence, we cannot compete with many countries.
4. We have spent too much on the military and ignore our crumbling infrastructure.
5. Historically no country can rule the world forever.
6. We blame China, but ignore how hard working Chinese are.

An example

This example evaluates RING, a gold miner, using ETFdb and Finviz that are free from the web. The data is from July, 6, 2020.

Bring up ETFdb and enter RING in the search. There are basic info that are important to me: Sector (gold miners), Asset Size (Large-Cap), Issuer (iShares), Inception (Jan. 31, 2012), Expense Ratio (0.39%) and Tax Form (1099).

They fit all my requirements. The expense ratio is higher than most ETFs that simulate an index such as SPY. I try to trade ETFs using Tax Form 1099 in my taxable accounts. The large cap created about 8 years ago by a reputable company is good.

Select "Dividend and Valuation". P/E of 17.39 is fine in a rank of 11 in 27 in a similar group of ETFs. As in my books, I stated it is hard to evaluate miners. I buy this ETF primarily to fight the possibility of inflation and the potential depreciation of USD. The dividend rate of 0.52% (0.70% from Finviz) is in the low range of the scale; it is fine for me as dividend is not my concern.

There is more info from this website. For simplicity, bring up Finviz:
- The short-term trend is up (SMA-20% = 8% and SMA-50% = 7%).
- The long-term trend is up (SMA-200% = 26%).
- It is close to overbought (RSI(14) = 64%; 65% to me is overbought).
- It is -4% from 52-w High. It has performed well from the YTD, Last Year, Last Quarter, Last Month and Last Week.
- It almost doubled in price from mid-March this year.
- Avg. Vol. is fine.

From ETFdb, check the Holding. It has 39 stocks, so it is quite diversified for this industry. The two top holdings are NEM (19%) and ABX (18%), which is listed as GOLD in NYSX. I also consider buying these two stocks in addition to RING. You can estimate the other metrics that are not available by averaging these two stocks. Here is my summary:

STOCK	NEM	GOLD
Forward P/E	20	25
Debt / Share	0.31	0.24
ROE	17%	22%
Sales Q/Q	43%	30%
EPS Q/Q	389%	254%
SMA50	2%	4%
RSI(14)	59%	60%
Insider Trans	-13%	N/A

Fidelity's Equity Summary Score	6.1	6.8

3 Rotate four ETFs

We can beat the market by rotating one ETF that represents the market such as SPY and cash via market timing. Aggressive investors can add SH or PSQ (contra ETFs) to the four to have better returns during market plunges.

During a market uptrend, rotating the following four ETFs could be more profitable than staying with SPY (or any ETF that simulates the market). Be warned that a short-term capital gain in taxable accounts is not treated as favorably as the long-term capital gain; check current tax laws.

The allocation percentages depend on your individual risk tolerance. You can use indexed mutual funds. Compare their expenses and restrictions. Some mutual funds charge you if you withdraw within a specific time period.

Select the best performer of last month (from Seeking Alpha, cnnFn, or one of many ETF/mutual fund sites). Add a contra ETF such as SH to take advantage of a falling market for more aggressive investors. Add sector ETFs to the described four ETFs such as XLY, XLP, XLE, XLF, XLU, IYW, XHB, IYM, OIL and XLU to expand your selection.

ETFs	Money Market	U.S.	International	Bond
Fidelity		Spartan Total Market	Spartan Global Market	Spartan US Bond
Vanguard		Total Stock Market	Total International Market	Total Bond Market
My choice	Fidelity	SPY	Vanguard	Fidelity
Suggest %				
During Market plunge	90%	0%	0%	10%
After plunge	10%	60%	20%	10%

Explanation

- The above are suggestions only. If your broker offers similar ETFs, consider using them.
- Check out any restrictions of the ETFs and commissions.
- 4 ETFs (one actually is a money market fund) are enough for most starters. They are diversified, low-cost and you do not need rebalancing except during a market plunge.
- The percentages are suggestions only. If you are less risk tolerant, allocate more to a money market fund, CD and/or bond ETF.
- Have at least 10% allocated to the money market fund for safety.
- When the market is risky, reduce stock equities (i.e. increase money market and bond allocations).
- The symbols for Fidelity ETFs are FSTMX, FSGDX and FBIDX.
- The symbols for Vanguard ETFs are VTSMX, VGTSX and VBMFX.
- If you are more advanced, use additional sector ETFs to rotate. Also buy long-term bond funds (such as 30-year Treasury) when the interest rate is 10% or more.

#Filler: Glad to be an investor

After watching the following YouTube video, I am glad my parents did not push me to play piano and also glad I do not have any musical gene. How can I compete with this kid?

https://www.youtube.com/watch?v=yf0B4rVoq44

Also glad not into some life-threatening professions such as surgical doctors, soldiers, fire fighters, etc. I can make mistakes in investing from time to time without suffering from the consequences. With the uptrend market for most of the last 50 years, most investors should make good money. Thank God.

4   Simplest way to evaluate stocks

Beginners should trade ETFs only. This chapter is for the readers who are ready or getting ready to trade stocks. In general, ETFs are diversified, less volatile than trading stocks. However, stocks offer higher profit but higher risk.

Many stock researches have already been done recently and some are available free of charge. I have no affiliation with Fidelity except I retired from it. You can open an account with them with no balance. Their Equity Summary Score is one of the best indicators; I check out **value** stocks with scores higher than 8. Concentrate on fundamental metrics such as P/E for long-term holds, and momentum metrics for short-term holds. Add criteria to limit the number of screened stocks. Finviz.com is a free screener.

Several sources

The popular ones are Morningstar, Value Line, The Street and Zacks (currently free for rankings of individual stocks). If they are not free, check out whether they are available from your local library. I have 3 simple ways to evaluate stocks starting with the simplest. In addition, read the articles on the selected stocks from Fidelity, Finviz, Seeking Alpha and many other sources for further evaluation.

Fidelity

Select only stocks that have Fidelity's Equity Summary Score 8 or higher. There is tons of information about a stock. Once in a while I did not agree with this score such as SHOP and ZM that scored high in August, 2020. Include the following for your analysis.

A modified stock selection based on a magazine article

Most metrics are available from Finviz except EV/EBITDA.

1. Forward P/E (expected earnings and not based on the last twelve months). It should range from 5 to 15 (10 to 25 for high tech stocks). EV/EBITDA (from Yahoo!Finance) is a better choice as it includes the debts and cash than P/E; it would be more effective if it uses forward earnings. If you do not use EV/EBITDA,

ensure Debt/Equity is less than 0.5 except for the debt-intensive industries.

2. ROE (Return of Equity) measures how well the company uses the capital. I prefer stocks with ROE greater than 5%.

3. Volatility. Conservative investors should select stocks with a beta of less than one (i.e. less volatile).

4. Insider Transactions for sales (i.e. negative) should be less than 5%. If it is -5%, most likely the insiders are dumping it.

5. Compare the metrics such as P/E and Debt/Equity to its five-year average and its competitors (available in Fidelity).

6. Momentum. Check out the SMA-50 (actually SMA-50%) and SMA-200. Ideally they should be positive. SMA-50% is especially important for stocks you do not want to keep for a long time.

7. Check out articles on the stock as some recent events (for example a new lawsuit) have not been included in the metrics.

8. Compare the trend of the sector this stock is in. Under Finviz, enter the related sector ETF.

Summary
The sources are Fidelity (Equity Summary Score and various comparisons), Finviz and Yahoo!Finance (for EV/EBITDA). Value stocks should be held longer.

Category	Score / Metric	Value /Momentum
Score	Fidelity's Equity Summary Score	Both
Value	EV/EBITDA	Value
	P/E cheaper compared to 5-year avg.	Value
	P/E cheaper compared to its sector.	Value
	Insider Purchases	Both
Safety	Debt/Equity	Value

	Compare it to its sector.	Value
Momentum	50-SMA%	Momentum
	200-SMA% (for long term holds).	Value
Articles	Check out latest events	Both
Market	No purchase if market is risky.	Momentum

A simple scoring system using Finviz
Bring up Finviz.com and then enter the stock symbol.

No.	Metric	Good	Bad	Score
1	Forward P/E[1]	Between 2.5 and 12.5, Score = 2	> 50 or < 0, Score = -1	
2	P/ FCF[1]	< 12, Score = 1	>30 or < 0, Score = -1	
3	P/S[1]	< 0.8, Score = 1	< 0, Score = -1	
4	P/ B[1]	< 1, Score = 1	< 0, Score = -1	
	Compare quarter to quarter of last year			
5	Sales Q/Q	> 15%, Score = 1	< 0, Score = -1	
6	EPS Q/Q	> 20%, Score = 1	< 0, Score = -1	
			Grand Score	
	Stock Symbol Date[2]	Current Price	SPY	

Footnote
[1] Negative values for Sales (due to accounting adjustments), Equity and Book are possible but not likely.
[2] The last row is for your information only. SPY is used to measure whether it will beat the market by comparing the return of this stock to the return of SPY.

The Score
Score each metric and sum up all the scores giving the Grand Score. If the Grand Score is 3, the stock passes this scoring system. Even if it is a 2, it still deserves further analysis if you have time. You may want to add scores from other vendors. To illustrate on using

Fidelity, add 1 to the score if Fidelity's Equity Summary score is 8 or higher. Monitor the performance after every 6 months or so to see whether this scoring system beats the market.

Very basic advice for beginners

Beginners should stick with U.S. stocks with Market Cap greater than 800 M (million), Debt/Equity less than .25 (25%) except for debt-intensive industries such as utilities and airlines and Forward P/E between 5 to 20 (25 for high-tech companies). These metrics are all available from Finviz.com, which is free.

Do not have more than 20% of your portfolio in one stock (unless it is an ETF or mutual fund) and do not have more than 30% of your portfolio in one sector.

For more conservative investors, buy non-volatile stocks whose beta (available from Yahoo!Finance) is less than 1. Beta of 1 represents the market (the S&P 500 index). For example, a stock with beta 1.5 statistically fluctuates more than 50% of the market and hence it is very volatile.

Try paper trading to check out your strategy and your skill in trading stocks. If your broker does not provide one, use a spreadsheet to record your trades or check the availability of simulator.investopedia.com.

#Filler: Silence is golden

I am glad I did not give advice to a friend who had to decide whether to take a lump sum payment or an annuity. The correction in March, 2020 would wipe out a lot of his portfolio if he took the lump sum payment. No one would share his profits when the predictions are correct, but the blame if it does not materialize.

It is the same in investing that nothing is certain. With educated guesses, we should have more rights than wrongs especially in the long run.

5   Simplest technical analysis

When the stock, the sector that the stock is in and the market are all above its SMA-N averages (Single Moving Average for the last N sessions), most likely the stock is trending up.

1. Bring up Finviz.com from your browser.

2. Enter SPY. Write down the SMA-200 (Single Moving Average for 200 sessions). Positive numbers indicate that the trend for the market is up.

    However, the market could be peaking or overbought. Be careful when SMA-200 is over 5% and / or RSI(14) is over 65%. RSI is a metric on over bought / under bought.

3. Enter the sector ETF the stock is in. Write down the SMA-50. Positive numbers indicate that trend for the sector is up.

    However, the sector could be peaking or overbought. Be careful when the SMA-200 is over 10% and / or RSI(14) is over 65%.

4. Enter the stock symbol. If your average holding period of the stocks is 200, use SMA-200 and so on. I recommend SMA-200 for holding value stocks long term and SMA-50 for momentum stocks. Write down the SMA-N for your stock. Positive numbers indicate that the trend is up.

    However, the stock could be peaking or overbought. Be careful when the SMA-200 (or SMA-50) is over 25% and / or RSI(14) is over 65%.

If the above three criteria and the fundamental criteria are satisfied, most likely it is a good buy. If you buy sector ETFs or mutual funds only, you can skip step #4. In any case, use stop loss to protect your investment.

#Filler: The Ten Commandments of Investing.
http://www.investopedia.com/articles/basics/07/10commandments.asp

* Set goals. * Personal finances in order. * Ask questions. * Do not follow the herd. * Due diligence. * Be humble. * Be patient. * Be moderate. * No unnecessary churning. * Be safe. * Do not follow blindly.

6   The best strategy

The best-kept secret in investing is to buy a weighed ETF. I use SPY as an example here. This ETF is well diversified as it keeps all 500 stocks in the S&P 500 index. The ETF has higher position (in percentage) on stocks with higher market cap. The stocks with higher market caps usually grow the market cap by having good management and good products. The bad stocks are deleted from the index periodically.

The second best-kept secret is using simple market timing as described in this book to reduce the losses in market crashes.

It is very hard to beat this strategy. You do not need any knowledge in investing, and you only spend a few minutes every month to time the market. The market is risky when the metrics show you so such as the price is close to the simple moving average in using SMA-350 method; in this case you time the market more frequently.

7   Don'ts for beginners

- Do not use leverage: options, margin and leveraged ETFs.
- Do not short stocks.
- Buy low and sell high.
- Buy value stocks. Sell profitable stocks after a year and losers before holding 12 months for favorable tax treatments in non-retirement accounts. Be a turtle investor.
- Limit momentum trades.
- Use stops to protect your portfolio.
- Do not follow 'experts' blindly (most have their own agenda).
- Do not trade penny stocks (i.e. stocks less than 200 M and/or price less than $1 to my definitions).
- Venture into momentum trading when you have knowledge and time. Avoid trading systems that are available.
- Do not day trade. Most beginners lose most of their money.
- Do not take classes / seminars that promise you big money - if it works, they will give out their secrets.
- Be selective on investing subscriptions. If they give you a handful of stocks to thousands of subscribers, most likely the actual performance will not be good. Check their past performances that use real money.

8   Summary

The following improves the odds of success but there is no guarantee.

Risky Market?
Bring up Finviz.com. Enter SPY. If both SMA-50% and SMA-200% are both negative, do not invest especially when SMA-50% is more negative than SMA-200%.

Evaluate value stocks from others' researches
Gather a list of stocks from screens and/or recommendations from magazines. Use researches that are free. Value stocks should be kept for at least 6 months. In six months or so, evaluate the bought stocks again to see whether you want to sell the stocks. Some other sites may provide free trial or one-time evaluation: IBD, GuruFocus, Zacks and Morningstar. Fidelity requires an account but there is no minimum position.

Name	Pass Grade	Link
Fidelity's Equity Summary Score	>=8	
Value Line[2]	Timeliness > Average	
	Proj. 3-5 yr.% > 5%	
VectorVest[1]	VST > 1 and RV > 1	Link

1   Should be available from your local library.

2   Free for limited number of stocks and free trial.

Evaluate stocks
Bring up Finviz.com and enter the stock symbol.

Metric	Passing Grade
Forward P/E	Between 5 and 20 (25 for tech stocks)
P/FCF	< 15 and ratio is positive
Sales Q/Q	>10
EPS Q/Q	>15

Intangible Analysis
Bring up Finviz, Fidelity, Yahoo!Finance or Seeking Alpha (fewer articles now) and enter the stock symbol. To prevent manipulation,

the stocks should have larger cap (> 200 M) and higher daily average volume (> 10,000 shares).

Bonus: Simplest way to detect correction

Corrections are hard to detect, hence beginners can ignore this article for now. When the market dips temporarily, it could be the best time to buy. When the market surges temporarily, it could be the best time to sell. Get a list of value stocks to buy and have cash ready. It works great in a sideways market. However, when the market plunges, do not buy any stocks. A correction could lead to a market crash.

How

Technical indicators may detect whether the market is ripe for temporary dips. On the average, I estimate there are two dips a year, but this number fluctuates widely. If the price is far higher than the SMA, it may be peaking for that period. RSI(14), the relative strength index using the last 14 days, determines whether the stock is overbought. It is not always reliable.

1. Bring up Finviz.com from your browser.
2. Enter SPY (an ETF simulating the S&P 500 index) on "Search Ticket".
3. SMA-200%, Single Moving Average for 200 days, indicates how far away the current stock price is from the SMA-200.
4. The market is peaking when SMA-200 is over 5%.
5. RSI(14) can be located in the right hand side of the metrics. The market is overbought when RSI(14) is over 65%.
6. When the P/E is greater than 25 (the average is 15), the market may be overvalued. Get it from http://www.multpl.com/
7. Suggested Actions:
   1. Do not buy stocks including ETFs when a correction is expected as indicated by these two conditions (#5 and #6).
   2. Do not want to exit the market totally as the market still could head higher.
   3. Sell some stocks that have reached your objectives. Do not sell more than 25% of your portfolio.
   4. Use trailing stops on the remaining stocks you bought. I recommend that you use 5% less than the current prices and 10% for volatile stocks. Adjust the stops accordingly every month.

5. If you trade SPY or other ETFs stocks instead of stocks, skip the following.
6. When the correction materializes and the reverse conditions occur (i.e. 5% is less than the last peak and/or RSI(14) is less than 30%), buy the ETFs and/or the stocks in your buy list.

Go back to step #1.

Bonus: Investing for 'lazy' folks

You have better things to do than investing or you do not have the time, the desire to learn and/or expertise in investing. You should be better off to buy ETFs.

I recommend the following 4 ETFs. If you have $100,000 to invest, buy $25,000 for each recommended ETF. Consult your financial advisor before taking any action. The recommended ETFs should have a large market cap (the ETFs themselves and not the stocks they hold) and have a high volume.

Most returns started on July 1 and ended on July 1 the following year; this article is written on July 20, 2021. All are annualized returns for easy comparison. Fees, commissions and dividends have not been included; you can add the dividend yield and prorate it for YTD return.

Symbol	Name	YTD[1] Return	1 Year[2]	5 Years[3]	Bear[4]
IWF	Russel 1000G	30%	34%	40%	-33%
QQQ	QQQ	30%	46%	42%	-31%
VTI	Vang. Viper Tot	34%	22%	42%	-35%
VUG	Vang. Growth	37%	33%	41%	-32%
Avg.		31%	34%	41%	-33%
SPY[5]		34%	21%	39%	-35%
Beat[6]		**-9%**	**60%**	**6%**	**7%**

[1] The start date is 1/4/2021 and the end date is 7/1/2021.
[2] The start date is 7/1/2020 and the end date is 7/1/2021.
[3] The start date is 7/1/2016 and the end date is 7/1/2021.
[4] The start date is 1/2/2008 and the end date is 4/1/2009. My estimates.
[5] SPY is the ETF for the S&P 500 index. It is used as a yardstick.
[6] = (Avg. − SPY) / SPY. Again it does not include fees, commissions and dividends.

Comments:

- The YTD is the only period that this portfolio does not beat SPY (the market to many). It could mean the market could be changing the favorite from growth stocks to value stocks. However, 31% return is far above the average of the market.
- The one-year return beats the market by 60%.
- The 5-year return beats SPY only by 6%, but the return of 41% is nothing to sneeze at.
- All except Vanguard's Viper Total are ETFs for growth stocks. Hence, I expected it would not beat the market, but it still did by 7%.
- You can time the market using the techniques described in this book as often as you can. When the indicator tells you to exit, you can sell these ETFs and reenter the market when it recovers. Riskier investors can buy contra ETFs such as PSQ and SH instead of holding cash when the market is down.
- At least once in a year review the selection. Use ETFdb.com for information. If you do not have time, it is fine skipping the review. When you switch ETFs, taxes should be considered.
- Most ETFs replace some stocks periodically to ensure better appreciation potential.

Bonus: Sample portfolio

It is a suggested sample. You need to tailor it to fit your personal requirements and your risk tolerance. In general, you should have an emergency fund for at least 3 months (6 months preferred). Many of our generation have one or even no layoff. However, I estimate the current generation will have 3 layoffs in their work life. It is due to automation, artificial intelligence, global economy, etc.

The rough estimate of stock holding in distribution between stock and bond is equal to 100 – Your Age. To illustrate in the following three portfolios, I use a 30-year old, and hence he should have 70% in stocks and 30% in bonds (including gold, CDs and cash).

In addition, some sectors are better than others according to the market conditions. The following three portfolios are for regular, todays' market and one during a market crash. I use low-cost ETFs exclusively. ETF is exchange-traded funds. They are traded similar to stocks, but most are more diversified; their fees are usually lower than mutual funds.

ETF	Normal	Today (2/2021)	Crashing[5]
SPY[1]	40%	30%	0%
QQQ[2]	5%	10%	0%
ARKK[2]	5%	0%	0%
VTIAX[3]	20%	5%	0%
LQD[3]	15%	20%	5%
GLD	5%	15%	15%
CD	5%	0%	0%
Cash	5%	20%	60%[6]
SH[4]	0%	0%	5%
PSQ[4]	0%	0%	15%

[1] VOO is a low-fee alternative for SPY.

[2] QQQ has more tech stocks, while ARKK is an actively managed ETF specializing in 'disruptive technologies'. During market crashes, avoid them.

[3] VTIAX is an ETF for global companies. LQD is an ETF for corporate bonds.

[4] SH and PSQ are contra ETF to SPY and QQQ. They are shorting the corresponding index. When the market is recovering, switch them back to SPY and QQQ.

[5] Need to balance the allocations about two times a year as ETFs can grow or shrink. When the market crashes, rebalance it right away. All markets will crash, and the last two (2000 and 2008) have an average loss of about 45%. Refer to the chapter "Simplest marketing timing".

[6] Today's low interest rate does not benefit us for CDs. I would leave the cash not invested and wait for the recovery to move back to stocks.

Of course, everyone's situation is different. If you are conservative, do not buy SH and PSQ. If you are afraid of inflation (especially due to the excessive printing of money), allocate more on GLD, a gold ETF.

Do not listen to financial news. They are used by institutional investors / analysts to manipulate the market. Many times they act the opposite from what they preach. This is the primary reason retail investors do not do better. With the GameStop incident, do not invest in most hedge funds. Buffett has proved the hedge funds with their high fees cannot buy an indexed ETF such as SPY.

The above is my recommendation. In the long run, it should work fine. Consult your financial advisor before taking actions. Most info is from RainIsHere, a Cantonese YouTuber.

#Filler: Simple measures to reduce net security.
Do not click any links from unknown sources. Some seem to be ok but not. MalwareBytes, for checking viruses, is free for download (they do not pay me). Personally I use a Chromebook for my financial transactions and a two-factor login for my stock trading.

#Filler "How to make a 50% return"

https://www.youtube.com/watch?v=eEto5nEkf1Y

#Filler Buffett, the person.
https://www.youtube.com/watch?v=w-eX4sZi-Zs

Section II: Finding Stocks

1   Where the web sites are

- **Free and simple screen sites**

    They are described in this article or type the following
    http://stocks.about.com/od/researchtools/a/071909screenlist.
    htm

    - Yahoo!Finance.
      Click here or type
      http://screener.finance.yahoo.com/stocks.html

    - Finviz.
      Click here or type
      http://Finviz.com/screener.ashx

      How to scan using Finviz (YouTube).
      https://www.YouTube.com/watch?v=aQ_0FTg9Cfw

      Screening using technical indicators.
      https://www.YouTube.com/watch?v=RZRP2NeSX0s

    - Your broker.
      Fidelity's screens are more sophisticated than most.

    - More options: Google, CNBC.com and Moringstar.com.

    Here is a list.
    http://stocks.about.com/od/researchtools/a/071909screenlist.
    htm

- **Sophisticated screens (these are usually not free)**
    Both Vector Vest and Stock123 provide historical databases for
    back testing your screens. Zacks has an earnings revision
    database at an extra cost. GuruFocus has an easy-to-use but
    powerful screen function. AAII provides screened stocks in its
    low-priced subscription. Both AAII and Value Line take care of
    some specific industries but they provide no historical database

at least for regular subscriptions. AAII provides historical performance summaries of their screens.

2 Fidelity

Fidelity offers a strong screen function. The most unique feature is incorporating its Equity Summary Score (used to be Analyst Opinion) and some outside researches such as Zacks and Ford.

From the main menu, select "News and Research", "Screen and Filter" and then "Start a screen".

The following example selects stocks with the following criteria: Security Price (2 to 250), Market Cap. (300 and above), Equity Summary Score (8 and above), Zacks (Strongest) and Ford (Strongest).

It displays the 10 stocks. Research each stock. Read the News about each stock. You may want to use Finviz.com, Yahoo!Finance and other sources to evaluate the stock again.

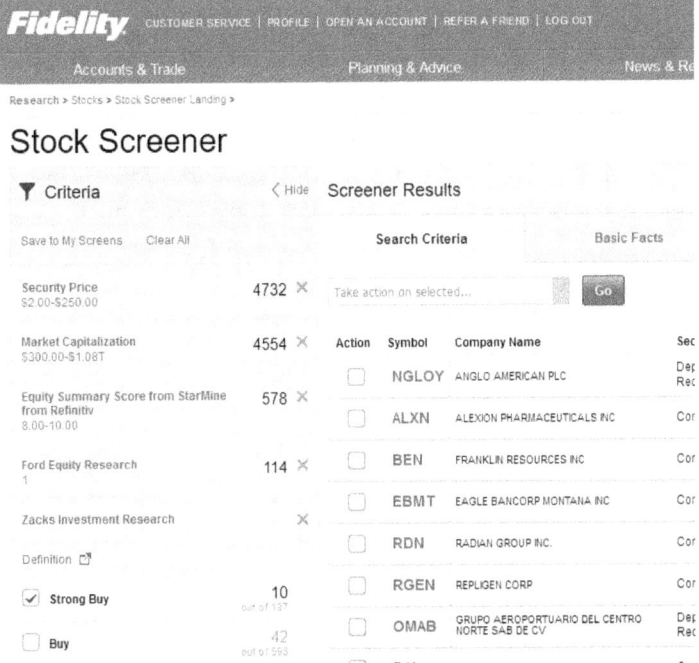

The Equity Summary Score (Analyst Opinions) has been proven to be a good predictor to me. The following describes some of the features.

- Equity Summary Score. It is one of the major metrics I use in my proprietary scoring systems. They do not track a lot of small stocks. From my limited database in 7/2015 and for short durations, the results are:

Short Term: (7% return for the average)

Metric	Parm. 1	No. of Stocks	%		Parm. 2	No.	%	Predicta-bility
Fidelity Analyst	Buy	150	10%		Sell	279	3%	Good

Long Term: (8% return for the average)

Metric	Parm. 1	No. of Stocks	%		Parm. 2	No.	%	Predicta-bility
Fidelity Analyst	Buy	90	17%		Sell	208	4%	Good

It has its own limits but they are very minor to me.

First, it does not have a historical database for verifying the screen performance such as the return after a year. However, I do not know any site that provides this function free. To work around this, I save the results in a spread sheet and update the performance.

Secondly, it does not provide many other filter criteria that can be found in other systems such as technical indicators or insider transactions found in Finviz.com. I copy the screened stocks to other sites for further evaluation.

Most investors should find that this screening is a very good tool and very easy to use.

3   Finviz.com screener

You should use fundamental metrics for fundamental stocks, growth metrics for growth stocks, momentum metrics for momentum stocks, and a combination. Basically you want to keep the fundamental stocks longer so the market would realize their values.

Finviz.com provides a screening function incorporating both fundamental and technical metrics and is one of the best free sites. Bring up Finviz.com in your browser and select screener. You have 4 tabs: Descriptive, Fundamental, Technical and All.

Besides incorporating technical indicators, it has the following features:

- The criteria specified can be saved.

- The searched stocks can be saved in a portfolio (for paper trading and performance monitoring).

- For an extra fee, you can have a historical database. This would help you to test your strategies.

- Some advanced technical indicators work well especially useful in momentum trading.

- Use technical patterns. My favorites are Head and Shoulder and Double Bottoms (Peaks). Use fundamental metrics to narrow down your selection.

Candlesticks is hard to master. Click the link for an introduction. You need to read a book dedicated to it and practice before you use it with real money. Misusing this technical indicator would cost you a lot of harm.

http://www.investopedia.com/terms/c/candlestick.asp

However, Finviz's screener lacks the following features:

- Stocks with prices trending up in the last several weeks (such as increasing X% in the previous week and y% in the week before the previous week, etc.). Use SMA-50% (or SMA-200 depending on your average time to keep the stock) for individual stocks after the search.

- Using exponential moving averages that supposedly have better predictive power than simple moving averages for momentum investing.

- Selecting ranges (for example, it cannot select all three major exchanges, market cap ranges, etc.).

- P/E for an ETF. It can be obtained from Yahoo!Finance.

- When the earnings (E) is negative, you may have the wrong values for P/E and the metrics using E. Some sites may have null values for negative earnings. For example, if you want stocks with P/E less than 20, the screener returns you stocks with negative earnings.

###
___

Here are three articles on using Finviz.com's screener.

Investopedia.
http://www.investopedia.com/university/features-of-Finviz-elite/other-chart-features.asp

How to scan using Finviz (YouTube).
https://www.YouTube.com/watch?v=aQ_0FTg9Cfw

Screening using technical indicators (YouTube).
https://www.YouTube.com/watch?v=RZRP2NeSX0s

###
___
A screener example

The following is an example. Fine-tune the selection criteria according to your personal criteria and risk tolerance.

- Bring up Finviz.com from your browser. Select Screener, the third tab. As of 3/24/2015, we have 7066 stocks.

- For illustration purposes, we would like to find stocks with double bottoms, a positive technical indicator. If not using the All tab, select the Technical tab. Select Pattern and then Double Bottom. Now we have 257 stocks.

- Select the Fundamental tab (next to the Technical tab). Select Forward P/E and then select "under 20". Now, we have 86 stocks.

- Select Debt/Equity less than .5. Now, we have 45 stocks. Some industries are traditionally high in debt, so you can use 'less than 1'.

- Select EPS growth Q-to-Q over 10%. Now, we have 19 stocks.

- Select the Description tab. Select Country to USA. Now, we have 17 stocks.

- Select Price > 1. Select Avg. Volume "Over 100K". Select Float Short "Under 10%. Select Analyst Recs. "Buy or better". Now we have 9 stocks.
  Now we can evaluate them one by one using Fundamental Analysis, Intangible Analysis, Qualitative Analysis and Technical Analysis. The purpose of screening is to filter the 7000 stocks to a small number (9 stocks in this case).

Skip the stocks that have the Earnings Date within 2 weeks. If you already have too many stocks in the same industry, skip that stock. You can save the screen when you register with Finviz.com. It is free. Check the performance in the last 3 months or so.
Other sources
Paper trade and check the actual performance before investing your money. Many popular screens and subscriptions worked before but may not work now. It could be too many folks are using the same strategy. Blue Chip Growth's ratings are positive from my recent monitor. I use GuruFocus.

Your broker

Most broker sites have screen facilities. Some have screens to simulate what a specific guru such as what Warren Buffett would do.

IBD

I recommend checking their recent performance vs. SPY. From my recent check on the IBD 50, they're good in the last 10 years, but not that good in the last 5 years – the victim of their own success perhaps? They provide stocks from their screens. Most screens are for momentum stocks and large caps. Here are the updated days for specific lists as of this writing. Check their result schedule.

Stocks Group	Published
Sector Leaders	Daily
Stock spotlight	Daily
Top World	Daily
IBD 50	Mon. and Wed.
Weekly Review	Fri.
Big Cap 20	Tue.

You may want to check out individual stocks with Stock Checkup and then analyze them again. The following are good parameters: Composite Rating, Industry Ranking (finer and better than Sector Ranking) and Relative Price. Understand their parameters and apply accordingly (the same for most other vendors).

IBD prefers large and growing companies with institutional ownership. Some of their parameters may not make sense for small, value and/or turn around companies.

Filler: Irresponsible is my best defense

I told my date that I would not be responsible after the second drink due to the lack of an enzyme.

Filler: Chicken feet, lobsters and trade war

Lobsters are literally flown to China for the rich. The trade war changes all these. Chicken feet, a delicacy for Chinese, will be thrown to the ocean. I can finally enjoy a $12 plate of lobster in Boston.

Common parameters

Different styles of investing use different parameters for screening stocks. Here is my summary/guideline on parameters in using Finviz.com. Finviz.com is not complete in all functions but it is the best free screener that incorporates both the fundamental and the technical criteria. The first table is for Value and the next one for Growth. The last one is for finding stocks the institutional investors are trading.

Value Screens	Common	Penny	Micro Cap	Dividend
General				
Market Cap (M)	>500	<50	50-200	+Mid(>2B)
Price	>5	< 5	1-15	>5
Exchanges (Major 3)	In	Not In	In	In
Avg. Volume	>100K	>5K	>10K	>100K
Country	USA		USA	USA
Dividend%				>3%
Float Short	<10%	<10%	<10%	<10%
Analyst Rec	Buy or +	Buy or +	Buy or +	Buy or +
Fundamental				
Forward P/E	<20	<20	<20	<25
ROE	>10	>10	>5	>15
QQ earning	>0			>0
QQ sales	>0			>0
PEG	<1	<1	<1	<1.2
Payout%				20-50%
P/S	<10	<10	<10	<10
Technical				
Price above 200 SMA	Yes	Yes	Yes	Yes
RSI(14)	Not Over	Not Over	Not Over	Not Over

There may be no analysts or very few following penny stocks and micro-cap stocks.

Growth

Growth Screen	Common	Technical	Momentum
General			
Market Cap (M)	>50	> 1,000	>500
Price	>1	>10	>5
Exchanges (Major 3)	In	In	In
Avg. Volume	>50K	>200K	>100K
Fundamental			
Forward P/E	<30	<30	<30
Return of Equity	>5	>0	>0
QQ earning	>10%	>15%	>20%
QQ sales	>5%	> 5%	>10%
PEG	<1	<1	<1
Analyst recs.	Buy or +		
Technical			
Price above 200 SMA	Yes	Yes	
50 SMA	Yes	Yes	Yes
RSI	< 75	< 75	

Short-term trends are important for momentum stocks.

Explanation

The above are suggestions only. Adjust them to your personal preferences and risk tolerance.

- Finviz screener lacks ranges, such as market cap and multiple of exchanges. To get around this, deselect the stocks that do not fit your requirements.

- Average Volume. When the price of the stock is less than $3, double the average volume requirement. In most cases, 10K is quite acceptable to me. When the volume is small, you may have to pay more (a.k.a. spread) to trade.

- There are many fundamental metrics such as Debt/Equity and Price/Free Cash Flow that are not included here but they should be included in your further evaluation. Each industry sector has different thresholds. For example, the P/S is very different for a supermarket rather than a high tech company. Compare the company to the average value of the companies in the same sector. Many sites including GuruFocus.com and Fidelity.com have the average values displayed.

- For momentum stock, you may ignore most of the fundamentals and concentrate on the price trend such as SMA-20% and SMA-50%. The higher the percent, the higher it is away from its own average. SMA-20 is the Single Moving Average for the last 20 trade sessions.

- For growth stocks, ensure the PEG (P/E growth), quarter-to-quarter earnings and quarter-to-quarter sales are above the averages in its own sector and/or the market.

- Technical analysis favors large cap stocks with large volumes. I prefer stocks with positive earnings and they are fundamentally sound.

- Include 3 basic technical indicators here. When they're all positive, they should be in an uptrend.

- RSI(14) indicates whether the stock is oversold (>60) or under bought (<35).
- You may want to check out your strategies using a virtual account from your broker or a simulator.

A general guideline for Institutional investors

Criteria	Value
Description	
Relative Volume	Over 2 M
Country	USA
Institution Ownership	Over 50%
Technical	
20-Day Simple Moving Avg.	>10%
Volatility	Week – Over 3%
RSI(14)	>40%
Fundamental	
Market Cap	>1B
ROE	>10%

- These are my suggested metrics and you may want to vary the parameters. I prefer USA companies. If you use foreign countries, ensure larger companies and/or in countries that have regulations similar to our SEC's.
- For value investors, select Forward P/E less than 20 (25 for high-tech companies) and that the Earnings are positive.
- Check out how many analysts are following the stocks that you are interested in.

To illustrate, I will find 12 stocks for that time frame. I narrow them down to 3. First, I skip all stocks that already have had more than 10% rise recently. They may have risen too high already.

Select profitable stocks with forward P/E less than 25. "Debt/Equity" is less than .5 (50%). Then, ROI is higher than 25%. Stop when you have reached the optimal number of stocks (2 for me in this example).

If you find too many stocks, tighten the criteria and vice versa. Save the criteria and the selected stocks in a portfolio for paper trading.

4   Finviz's parameters

Most metrics are described in Finviz (via Help), Investopedia and/or Wikipedia and my chapters on P/E and fundamental metrics if available. We use the metrics for screening stocks and then evaluating the screened stocks.

The following are my personal comments and why I feel some metrics are more important than the others. Personally I divide the metrics into fundamentals and technical, which are more important for long-term investors and short-term investors respectively.

Compare the ratios to the companies in the same sector (industry) and also its averages from the last few years (5 preferable) from many other websites such as Fidelity.

From your browser, enter Finviz.com. Enter a symbol (I used ABEO for discussion). A chart is displayed with the prices and volumes for the last eleven months. SMAs (Single Moving Average) are displayed sometimes with other technical indicators. Intraday, Daily and Weekly options are available for day traders, short-term traders and long-term traders respectively.

Besides the chart and the metrics described next, it describes what the company does, analysts' recommendations (I prefer Fidelity's Equity Summary), insiders' trading and articles that are good for intangible and qualitative analysis. Many free websites such as Yahoo!Finance may provide a list of articles about the company.

"Financial Highlights and Statements" are materials for more in-depth analysis and they were more important decades ago when most financial ratios had not been calculated for you. It is important for investors with good knowledge in financial accounting. The current version also includes basic financial statements and cash flow for the current (TTM) and the last two years.

A section on Insider Trading is also included. Do not be alarmed when insiders dump small quantities of the stocks. Buying large quantities (e.g. insider transaction more than 5%) at prices close to the market price could be favorable news.

The following metrics are roughly based on the flow of Finviz from top to bottom and left to right. I skip those metrics that I believe are not too important. You can also place your cursor on the metric to retrieve the description from Finviz. Some metrics are left blank to indicate they are not applicable (zero, negative or not available). For example, the Debt/Equity of YRCW in 1/2019 is blank (same as null) due to its negative Equity. From Yahoo!Finance at the time of writing, it has a total debt of 888M.

- **Index**. Most of us trade stocks in the three major exchanges in the USA. Stocks listed over-the-counter are too risky for most of us. Skip the stocks in local exchanges and foreign exchanges unless you are an expert on these stocks and/or have insightful (not insider) information. I screen the stocks and then ignore the stocks that are not in the Dow, NASDAQ and Amex. Other screeners may let you select a group of exchanges.

- **Market Cap** (MC). To me, stocks below 50M are risky even though they could be very profitable. Ensure the Avg. Volume is at least 10,000 shares and / or your order is less than 1% of the average volume. Some small stocks are controlled by the owners and have small volumes. In this case you cannot sell your stock easily.

  Float = Outstanding shares – Insider shares.

  Usually Float does not matter as they are typically the same. However, it does for small companies with large insider shares. Most of these owners do not want to sell their family businesses and hence they reduce the chance of being acquired entirely or partially for good prices. In this case, you may have to hold this stock for a long time or you sell it at a very unfavorable price.

- If **Forward P/E** (a.k.a. Expected P/E) is not provided, use the P/E which is based on the trailing last 12 months (TTM). Alternatively, calculate the E by using the E from P/E and multiplying it by its growth rate. It may not be seasonally adjusted. I prefer using Forward P/E as it provides a better predictability power to me.

  Finviz.com leaves the P/E blank (same as null) if the earnings are negative. In this case, I would check out Yahoo!Finance's EV /

EBITDA, which also considers taxes, cash and interests. The blank condition is similar to some metrics such as when the asset is negative (they seldom occur).

Earnings Yield is equal to E/P. I call it True Earnings Yield for EBITDA / EV. It is easier to understand. Compare Earnings Yield or True Yield to the annual dividend yield of a 10-year Treasury – with the low interest rate in 2021, skip the comparison.

E/P is easier in screening and sorting the screened stocks. If you use P/E instead of E/P, you need to screen or sort stocks with a clause "P/E > 0".

When the P/E is less than 5, be careful and there may be a reason why it is so low. Many bankrupting companies have low P/Es at one time.

Compare the P/E or Forward P/E with the average P/E for the sector and its average P/E for the last 5 years that are available from Fidelity.com. Some sectors have high P/Es. If the sector is cyclical, the earnings could be affected.

When the prospect of the company is good such as Tesla in 2020, ignore P/E.

- **Cash / share**. It is used to calculate Pow P/E and Pow EY when EV/EBITDA for the stock is not available. To illustrate, if the stock is $10 and it has $10 cash / share without debt (i.e. Debt/Equity = 0), most likely it is underpriced as you can get the whole company for nothing. You should find out why the price is so low. It could be the market ignoring the stock, or there is a serious event happening such as a major lawsuit.

- **Dividend %** is useful for income investors. The payout ratio should not be more than 30% except for matured companies. Most developing companies plough back the profits into research and development, and hence they do not pay dividends.

- **Recs**. Select stocks with 1 or 2. Do not base your stock selection on this recommendation alone. There have been many bad recommendations that could cost you a fortune in losses. Use Fidelity's Equity Summary Score instead.

- **PEG** is a measure of the growth of P/E and hence a growth metric. It is similar to P/E, but it takes the expected earnings growth rate into account. The lower value is better as long as earnings are positive. If earnings are negative, then the reverse is true. It is a defect in using P/E and PEG and that's why I recommend EY (Earnings Yield) and EYG, earnings yield growth.

  If there are two companies with the same P/E, the one with a better PEG ratio is better. If two companies have the same E/P, the company with higher Earnings Growth (EPS Q/Q) would be better for similar logic.

- **P/B**. Book value (= Total Assets − Total Liabilities) may not include intangible assets such as patents. Do not trust it 100%, so is ROE which is based on the book value. Negative equity is possible when Total Liabilities is more than Total Assets. This popular metric is outdated for most matured companies as it is now made up of more intangible assets including patents, management, the quality of their employees, brand names, market share, partners, free cash flow and customer base.

- **P/S**. If two companies are unprofitable, this ratio can be used. A retail company such as Walmart is very different from a research company. This metric is only meaningful for stocks within the same sector or specific sectors.

- **P/FCF**. I prefer it to be greater than 0 and less than 50 for value investors. Most metrics can be manipulated easily, but not this one.

- **Sales Q/Q** reduces the seasonal deviation. To illustrate, retail sales for the Christmas season should be compared to the same season in the prior year.

- **EPS Q/Q**. Same as above. I prefer the growth of EPS over Sales. Both of these Q/Q ratios are growth metrics. When a company terminates its unprofitable product(s), its Sales Q/Q could be down but its EPS Q/Q could be up. In 2000, many internet companies had great Sales Q/Qs but negative EPS Q/Qs.

Q/Q comparison (quarter to quarter) takes out the seasonal variations as Sales Q/Q. I prefer both Sales Q/Q and EPS Q/Q increase. When EPS Q/Q increases far higher than Sales Q/Q, it could mean the EPS Q/Q could be temporary such as the oil company when the oil price rockets.

When the company buys its own shares, EPS could be misleading as E is fixed and the number of shares is reduced. In most cases, the fundamentals of the company have not changed.

- Positive **Insider** Transactions are favorable. Sometimes, they are misleading. Need to scroll to the end of the screen and check out more info there. If the transactions are outdated such as 3 months or so ago, and or they are purchases in a similar amount than the sales a while ago, they are not important. Insiders know the company better than us. So is Institutional Transactions as institutional investors move the market.

- Insider Own, Shares Outstanding and Shares **Float** determine the number of shares that are available for trading. A small Float with a high Insider Own limits trading and the stock should be avoided in most cases. Compare your trade position for the stock to the Avg. Volume.

- **Profit Margin**. I prefer it over Gross Margin and Oper. Margin which does not include interest expenses and taxes. When you sell software, the Gross Margin is high as it does not include development, support and marketing, etc. A retail store has low Gross Margin. It all depends on the industry, and hence it is better to compare companies in the same industry.

- **Short Float**. I prefer it to be less than 10%. If it is greater than 10%, the shorters could find something wrong with the company. If it is over 25% (indicating a possible short squeeze), I would check the fundamentals. If they are good, I would buy expecting a short squeeze potential. It is risky but it has been proven to be profitable for me.

- Technical metrics: SMA-20, SMA-50 and SMA-200. Finviz expresses them in convenient percentages. If they are all positive, it means the trend is up. SMA-20 and SMA-50 are a short-term trend and SMA-200 is a long-term trend. If you are a short-term swing investor, stick with the short-term trend and vice versa. The first two are also used as momentum grades. Many long-term investors do not buy stocks when the SMA-200% is negative.

- **RSI(14)**. If it is greater than 65%, it is overbought. If it is under 30%, it is under-bought for me. Some use 5% up or down than mine. Use it as a reference. Most stocks making new heights are always overbought, and many of these stocks keep on rising. I recommend using trailing stops to protect your profit.
- **Beta**. A volatile stock fluctuates a lot. It is good for short-term traders. A beta of 1 means the stock would fluctuate with the market, and be volatile if it is higher than 1. For volatile stocks (higher than 1), the stops should be higher. For example, if your stops are normally 15%, you may want to use 20% or even higher.
- Management performance is measured by <u>ROE</u>. It is also judged by **Analysts' Rec.** and Institutional Ownership (except for small companies). The confidence of their own ability, the company and its sector is measured by Insider Ownership and Insider Purchases.

  ROE = Net Income / Average Shareholder's Equity
  According to Investopedia, a normal ROE for utilities should be 10% while high tech companies should be 15%. Compare this ratio and many other ratios with its peers that are available from Fidelity.
- Avoid all companies that are going to bankrupt at all costs. Debt/Equity, P/FCF, Cash/Sh., P/B, Profit Margin, Forward P/E, Short Float, RSI(14), SMA20% and SMA50 would give us hints. Need to summarize all the info and study many other factors such as obsoleting products (including drugs).
- Unless you have concrete information, do not buy stocks a week or so before the Earnings Date. It is seldom to make great profits when the announcement is better than the expected.

More useful information:

- The price chart. It has a lot of features such as the resistance line. Some charts include technical indicators such as double top (a bearish warning) and double bottom (a bullish sign).

- Description under the symbol. It briefly describes what the company (sector and industry) does and its country of registration. You want to buy a stock within a sector that is trending up. For example, according to Finviz Apple is in the Consumer Goods sector and the Electronic Equipment industry.

  If you do not want to buy foreign stocks, skip it if it is not listed in the US exchange.
- Articles on the company for qualitative analysis.
- Insider trading. Pay more attention to the insider purchases at market prices. Use common sense.
- The last line lets you open Yahoo!Finance and other sites.

Other important sites

Yahoo!Finance.

From Statistics, you can find Enterprise Value / EBITDA. I call it True Yield when I flip them to EBITDA / Enterprise Value.

In case it is not available, I use Earnings Yield. In my spreadsheet without considering the cell designations,

=IF (Earnings Yield = "", True Yield, Earnings Yield)

Fidelity

Compare the P/E of the average PE of the last 5 years. In my spreadsheet for demonstration,

Cheaper By Historically =IF(PE="","",(Avg. of 5-year PE -PE)/Avg. of 5-year PE)

Compare the P/E of companies in the same sector. In my spreadsheet for demonstration,

Cheaper By To the peers =IF(PE="","",(Industry PE - PE)/Industry PE)

Your broker's website

Your broker website should have plenty of tools to analyze stocks. As of Dec., 2018, Fidelity lets you use their extensive research free by opening an account with no position restriction. I describe some of their metrics that should be beneficial to your research.

- Equity Summary Score. Potentially good buy when it is 7 (8 for conservative investors) or higher. With some exceptions, you should avoid or short stocks if the score is 3 or below. The stocks ranking from 4 to 6 could be turnaround candidates if they are supported by good Q/Q Earnings and/or good news.

- The 5-year averages are good yardsticks. For example, in Dec., 2018, C's P/E is about 9 and the average is 14. Hence it is a value buy.

Other sources

If you have other sources (most require a subscription or being a customer), skip the stocks that have one of the failing grades. The exceptions are a new positive development and increased insider purchases.

Vendor	Grade	Fail
Fidelity	Equity Summary Score	< 7
IBD	Composite grade	< 50
Value Line	Proj. 3-5 yr. return. Also its composite rating	< 3%
Zacks	Rank	5
VectorVest	VST	< 0.7

You may be able to find Value Line and IBD in your library. Try out the free stock reports from your broker first. Finviz and Seeking Alpha should have articles (now fewer free articles from Seeking Alpha) on stocks and earnings conferences, which could have important information after separating from the "welcome" and garbage talks.

Yahoo!Finance has good info. "EV/EBITDA" is better than "P/E" as it considers debts and cash. Most use Earnings from last 12 months, which has poorer predictability than Forward Earnings to me.

When negative values such as Equity in Finviz.com, we need to adjust many related metrics or do not use them at all.

MarketWatch.com has many articles on the market in general and personal investing.

If the stock is close to the Earnings Date (found in Finviz.com), you should avoid trading the stock; as earnings could have a big swing for the stock price. Consult Zacks' ranking which is currently free for individual stocks.

Gurus

It is nice to know how gurus would rate the interested stocks. GuruFocus is a good source. NASDAQ is a simplified version, but it is currently free. Bring up Nasdaq.com from your browser. Select "Investing" and then "Guru Screeners". On the third selection, enter the stock symbol such as THO. Click "Go". You will find how 10 or so gurus would evaluate this stock in theory. Click "Detailed Analysis" for each guru.

Quick and dirty

Many times we need to evaluate a stock fast such as taking action due to some development. Refer to my other article "Simplest way to evaluate stocks". The following should take a few minutes. Bring up Finviz.com and enter the stock symbol.

Using SWKS on 6/10/16 to illustrate, Forward P/E is about 11 (fine between 3 and 25), Debt/Eq. is 0 (fine less than .5), ROE is 30% (fine greater than 5%) and P/PCF is 31 (fine if not negative).

Also, check out Market Cap, Avg. Volume, Dividend, Short Float (fine between 0% and 10%), Country and Industry. Judging from the above, it is a buy.

If you have more time, check out the following: Recom. (Ok if less than 2.5), P/B (fine between .5 and 4), Sales Q/Q (fine if not negative), EPS Q/Q (fine if not negative), Cash/Sh (compare it to Debt/Sh) and Profit Margin (fine >5%). Check some articles described for this stock.

5-minute stock evaluation

It takes even less time than the above "Quick and Dirty". However, I recommend you should spend more time researching stocks.

- From Finviz.com, enter the stock or ETF symbol. Look at the number of reds in metrics. If there are more than greens, most likely it is not a good stock.

- It should be fine if Fidelity's Equity Summary Score is greater than 8.

If you have more time, I recommend you to check the following:

- Check out Forward P/E (E>0 and P/E < 20), Debut / Equity (< 50%) and P/FCF (not in red color).

  If time is allowed, replace Forward P/E with True P/E (same as "EV/EBITDA"), which is available from Yahoo!Finance and other sources.

- SMA20 (or SMA50 for longer holding period). If SMA20 is > 10%, it is trending up.

- It is fine if the Insider Transaction is positive.
- Be cautious on foreign stocks and low-volume stocks.
- If most of the above are positive, it is likely a buy. As in life, nothing is 100% certain.

Links
PEG: http://en.wikipedia.org/wiki/PEG_ratio
Short %:
http://www.investopedia.com/university/shortselling/shortselling1.asp#a
xzz2LNDvpemo
Openinsider: http://www.openinsider.com/
Finviz: http://Finviz.com/
terms: http://www.Finviz.com/help/screener.ashx
Insider Cow: http://www.insidercow.com/
Current Ratio: http://en.wikipedia.org/wiki/Current_ratio
How to find quality stocks.
http://seekingalpha.com/article/2381395-how-to-identify-quality-stocks-and-is-there-really-alpha-to-be-had

5 A scoring system

This scoring system helps you to select whether you should buy a stock or not. In this system, when a stock scores higher than 2, it is a buy. As a group, the highly-scored stocks usually perform better than the lowly-scored stocks in a year. The basic concepts are described here.

An Example

For illustration purposes, we use two metrics: Forward P/E and ROI.

First we convert Forward P/E into Forward E/P by flipping the two values. Assuming Forward E/P should have a higher weight than ROI, multiply E/P by 5. The average ROI is 10% (simplified for illustration), so minus it by .1.

Score = Forward E/P * 5 + (ROI -.1)

For example, a stock has a P/E of 10 (E/P = 1/10= .1) and ROI is expressed as 25%.

Score = .1 * 5 + (.25 - .1) = .5 + .15= .65

Some parameters by some sites are expressed in grade such as A, B, C and D. For simplicity, if it is A, then the value is 2 otherwise it is zero.

Score = if (Grade = "A", 2, 0) + ...

Test your system on paper with at least 3 months of data. Check whether your scoring system works. It works when the higher the score corresponds to the better the return. Adjust the weight on each metric and see whether your scoring system improves its predictability.

Again, it is simplified for educational and illustration purpose. Try even more different metrics and check whether the metrics still work in the current market. The next metrics to include could be Equity Summary Score from Fidelity, Debt/Equity and Quarter-to-Quarter Earnings / Sales.

Monitor your scoring system

I am sure that many have tried to use most of the metrics and they still cannot find the Holy Grail. I believe the predictability power of each metric is influenced by the current market conditions. For example, the fundamental metrics such as P/E predict better than the growth metrics such as PEG during the market bottom. You should test the performance of each metric every 6 months or so.

You may have two scores: one for short term and one for long term. The stocks you want to keep in the short term may not be the same kind of stocks you want to keep in the longer term. Short term is 3 months (one month for me) and long term is 12 months for me. My definitions could be different than yours. Value metrics are more important for the long term while growth metrics are more important for the short term.

However, 12 months is too long a period of time and during this period the market may change, so it is better to change it from 12 to 6. To illustrate, energy stocks were great in 2007, but they plunged in 2008. If your scoring system for long-term holding was constructed based on 12 months' data in 2007, the system would have been misleading in 2008 for energy stocks in this example.

I find the short-term scores have a better prediction power than the long-term scores. However, I keep profitable stocks more than 12 months to qualify for the better tax treatments in taxable accounts, and sell the losers less than 12 months. Evaluate the purchased stocks every 6 months to decide whether you want to keep them for another 6 months. Use stops and trialing stops (for winners) to protect your portfolio.

Besides monitoring the metrics in your scoring system, monitor the scores.

The market is not always rational

Sometimes the scoring system fails: When the poorly-scored stocks perform better than the highly-scored stocks. The market is not always rational. Most scoring systems depend on fundamental metrics. When the market switches its favor from value to growth, adjust the score system accordingly. I have found that more than one time that the stocks scored in the top 5% did not perform, so be careful or skip the top 5% (sometimes 10%). The events such as a pending lawsuit or an expiring drug do not show up in metrics, and that is why we need to do other analysis such as Intangible Analysis.

Some metrics almost always work such as the positive predictions of excessive insider's purchases. The insiders know the company typically better than others. When they buy their own company's stock at market prices, they must know it has good appreciation potential. They have many reasons to sell their company's stocks. However, when they sell a large percent of their holdings, be cautious.

When the stock loses more than 30% in a month and you cannot find valid reasons, it may be a good indicator for potential appreciation ahead. Some suggestions are:

- Do not modify your scoring system during market plunges.
- The best strategy is to use the screens (same as searches) that have worked well for the last 90 days.
- Find out why your fundamental metrics that used to work do not work now. You may want to add more weight on growth metrics, and vice versa on value metrics.

An example of monitoring the metrics

This is what I found in monitoring the performances of the metrics as of 3/2013. It is based on a limited database of about 300 stocks with holding periods varying from 1 to 15 months. It has an average of 8% (16% for shorter term). The following is for educational purpose only.

1. The foreign stocks are not doing well: South America (average return is -21% for 7 stocks), Israel (-18% for 2), China (-10% for 7). Europe (0% for 17) and Canada (5% for 16, and most are in natural resources). If I ignore the foreign companies, the return of the portfolio would be increased substantially.

2. The following metrics work fine for the long term only: Forward (same as Expected) Earnings Yield (E/P) and Fidelity's Equity Summary Score.

3. P/B. The stocks with P/B less than 1 perform better than the stocks with P/B greater than 2 (10% vs. 4%).

4. There are no definitive conclusions on Cash / Market Cap, PEG and Return of Equity (a surprise to me) in this monitor.

5. The stocks that were cheaper by 50% to their average 5-year P/E (available from Fidelity) have performed better than those stocks that were cheaper by less than 2%.

6. The ratio of Short / Market Cap between 25% and 30% has better performance than other percentages. It is a contradictory ratio and it could be a short squeeze (a condition that the stock is running out of shares to sell short).

7. There are many composite scores from different vendors that I subscribe to and they are not disclosed here.

8. Based on the above, I will modify my scoring system. I will still have two scores, one for short term and one for longer term.

Short-term scoring system

The scoring system should work better in the shorter term. For testing this system, I used the above data base, but deleted stocks that have been over 8 months old. It is still a small data base of about 190 stocks.

The result is different from the above as the time frame has been reduced. Here is the summary.

1. The predictability of screens (same as searches) performs about the same as the last monitor. A few screens are better than others. I will not use the under-performing screens with real money.

2. The stock grades from several vendors are not a good indicator this time.

3. Expected (same as Forward) Earnings Yield (E/P) has been a good indicator.

4. Cash Flow is a good indicator (different from the last monitor).

5. Fidelity's Equity Summary Score is a good indicator. Finviz has a similar score, but I prefer to use Fidelity's. Fidelity places higher weight on opinions from analysts that have a better prediction on this stock than others. It eliminates some of the conflict of interest between the analysts and the investing banks s/he works for.

6. The Short Percentage between 25 and 30 is a good contrary indicator (could be a good chance for a short squeeze).

   Its value of less than 10 % is a good indicator. The rest of the range is not conclusive.

7. Cash / Market Cap, Insider Purchase, P/B, ROE and Dividend stocks (>3%) are not conclusive in this monitor.

8. P/S with values less than 0.8 are a good indicator.

9. For some reason I do not know why and how to explain: the top 10% of the top-scored stocks did not perform better than the other stocks that pass.

   It happens in both my two scoring systems. Be suspicious of them and it has happened for more than once. However, the stocks that scored in the bottom 10% are consistently poor performers and that's a good indicator.

There are many other parameters that may be of interest to you. Include them in the performance monitor.

6   Sectors to be cautious with

There are many reasons to be very cautious when investing in the following sectors. However, Technical Analysis (a.k.a. charting) would give you more hints than the fundamentals for stocks in these sectors.

Loan companies/banks

The financial statements do not show the quality of their loan portfolios. Following this advice, you may be able to skip the banks that melted down in 2007. The peak of Citigroup is $550 and several banks went bankrupt.

Drug (generic is ok)

Understanding the complexities of the drug pipelines, its potential profits for new drugs and the expiration of its current drugs may not be worth the effort for most retail investors. In addition, a serious lawsuit and / or a serious problem with a drug could wipe out a good percentage of the stock price. When a drug shows unpromising sign(s) in any trial phase, the stock could plunge and vice versa.

Miners

It is extremely difficult to estimate how much ore (sometimes a miner owns several different types of ores and/or of different grades in the same or different mines) that the company has. It is further complicated by the complexities to extract and transport them. When the total of these costs is greater than its production price, the company will not be profitable. Understanding the market for ore futures is another discipline.

Many mining companies are in foreign countries such as Canada, Australia and countries in South America. Their financial statements of Canada and Australia are more trustworthy than those from most other emerging countries.

One potential problem of mining companies from many emerging countries is nationalization.

Mining rare earth ore is extremely risky when the profit depends on how China, a major producer of these ores, will price its ores. After China announced the export restrictions on rare earth elements, several non-Chinese companies announced to reopen their mines for rare earths but few have made any profits as of 2013. Developed countries have stricter environmental regulations.

Coal suffers from the rising use of cleaner oil and gas.

Insurance companies

Insurance companies profit by:

1. The difference between the total premiums received and the total claims minus expenses in running the company.

2. How well they invest your premiums; you pay your premiums earlier than you may collect from the claims.

They can protect the profits in #1 by restricting claims by natural disasters such as earthquakes and by re-insuring. However, a bad disaster could wipe out a lot of their profits.

Even if the insurance company shows you its investment portfolio, most of us, the retail investors, do not have the time and expertise to analyze it.

Emerging countries (not a sector)

Their financial statements especially from small companies cannot be trusted and many countries use different accounting standards. Emerging countries are where the economic growth is. I trade FXI, an ETF, rather than individual Chinese companies. I have lost a lot in small Chinese companies due to fraud. To check out whether the stock is an ADR, try ADR.COM.

https://www.adr.com/

Stocks with low volumes (not a sector)

Most likely you pay a high spread to trade these stocks. They can be manipulated easier. I remember when I had a hard time trying to sell a stock of this kind. The majority of this company is owned by one person.

For simplicity, I trade stocks with the average daily trade volume over 6,000 shares (double it if the price is $2 or less). A better way could be in calculating the percent of your trade quantity / average daily trade volume to reduce the effect of penny stocks that have larger volumes due to the low prices. You need special skills to trade these stocks but it could be very profitable.

Good business and bad business

Banking is a good business. My deposit in them makes virtually zero interest, and they loan the same money making 3%. If they are more selective in loaning my money, they should make a good profit.

Restaurant is an easy business to open/run, but it is very hard to make good money. With the rising of minimal wages, it will get even tougher. That could be the reason for so many coupons today. The high-end restaurants are doing better due to the rising stock market. As of 8/2014, the new comers Noodles & Company (NDLS) and Potbelly (PBPB) are not doing very well.

Retailing is a tough business. Look at the top 10 retailers 15 years ago, I can only find two including Macy's that are still surviving. Most are either bankrupt or being acquired. Even Macy's was at one time in financial trouble.

Airlines are a tough business. You can tell by the average increase in fares in the last 10 years. It cannot even beat inflation. They have to charge you for everything. The next frontier charge is the rest room (especially for long-distance flights). Now I understand why they call themselves "Frontier Air".

There are several software companies that produce software such as the virus detecting programs and tax preparation software. The customers faithfully buy new versions every year. That's great business.

7 Intangibles

I give a score for each stock I evaluate. Occasionally some stocks with poor scores have great returns and vice versa. In general, the scoring system works and it has been proven statistically and repeatedly from my limited data.

I stick with high-score stocks with some exceptions and once in a while I change my scoring system to adept to the current market conditions. To illustrate, the market bottom phase and early recovery phase of the market cycle favor value more than momentum/growth. Here are some of my recent experiences and strategies:

- I double or even triple my stake on stocks with high scores. In the longer term, they are consistently better winners than the average with some minor exceptions. Besides the score, look at the intangibles described in this article.
- Watch out for the stocks with outrageous metrics such as P/E of 4 or less. It could be a big lawsuit pending, an expiration of some important drugs, etc. Also, be careful with scores in the top 5%. From my statistics they do worse than the average. Their problems may not show up in the current financial statements and hence the fundamental metrics do not reflect the problems. This could be the only part of the market efficiency theory that makes sense.

- The technology of a tech company cannot be ignored even though the company's P/E is high. The value of the company's technology and patents will not be shown in the fundamental metrics except from the insiders' purchases at the market prices.

  For example, IDCC rose about 40% in 2 days. There was a rumor that Google was buying the company and/or Apple was bidding on it too for its mobile technology. Charts usually would flag this kind of event. They could be a little late as the charts depend on rising prices.
- There are more acquisitions during a market bottom and early recovery. The companies with good technologies are bargains and the larger companies especially in the same sector understand their values better than most of us. These potentially profitable companies will not be shown by their scores explicitly. When corporations have a lot of cash or the

credit is cheap, they are looking for smaller companies to acquire or invest in. The candidates are usually small, beaten up, low-priced and having valuable intangible assets such as technologies, customer base and/or market share of the industry segment. 2009-2012 was just the perfect environment and the last one was 2003. I had at least one in each of these periods.

- The opposite is Netflix, Chipotle in 1/2012 and Amazon in 1/2013. They are over-priced by any measure. However, the shorters are having a tough time. I do not recommend selling short especially for novice investors. When their P/Es are higher than 40, watch out. Some could be OK, but usually they are not. Do not follow the herd and your due diligence will verify whether they will still go up.

   Use reward/risk ratio. It is based on experiences. To illustrate, if the company has the equal chance to go up 50% and go down 25%, then it is a buy and the reverse is a sell.

- The retail investor just cannot possibly know about some events until they actually happen. For example, ATSC dropped 15% due to losing its second primary customer. Fundamentals cannot predict this kind of any event. Charts can but usually they are too late unless you watch the chart all day long. Some subscription services indicate these stocks in a timely fashion.

- After a quick run up, TZOO plunged due to missing some negligible earning expectations. It seems the original climbing prices already had the perfect earnings growth built-in.

   I do not understand why a company loses 10% of its market cap when it missed by 1% of the expected earnings. It could be driven up and down by the institutional investors. Evaluate the stock before you act. Acting opposite of the institutional investors could be very profitable for the right stocks. Avoid trading before the earnings announcement dates (about 4 times a year for most stocks).

- The following are not easily found in financial statements: industry outlook, patents, good will, market share, competition, product margins, management quality, lawsuits pending, potential acquisition, pension obligations, advertising icons, etc. That is why we need to read articles on the stocks in our buy list.

- The financial data could be fraudulent or manipulated. I do not trust small companies in emerging markets. I have been burned too many times. Check the company names such as foreign names, ADR... and their headquarter addresses (from the company profile in most investing sites) to start with.

  Earnings can be manipulated with many accounting tricks. A jump in earnings from last year may not be as rosy as it looks. Check the footnotes in the accounting statements. I usually skip financial statements unless I have big purchases in mind.

- Cash flow cannot be easily manipulated. It is good information whether the company will survive or not, but to me it does not prove to be a consistent predictor in my tests, but an important red flag for companies on their way to bankruptcy. There have been many examples.

- Repeated one-time, non-recurring and extraordinary charges are red flags. For a limited test for the average of "these charges / sales" for 2007 and 2008, I grouped them into 1. The average is over 25% (AVB, AWK and Y) and 2. The average is less than 5% (CAT, DIS, ADBE and AMAT). The average annualized returns are:

	1 yr. (2009 to 2010)
Group 1	14%
Group 2	38%
SPY	22%

- The data is too limited for a conclusion. However, when the average of the last two years is over 25%, you need to further evaluate the stocks and find out the reasons.
- Stay away from the companies where the CEOs are over-compensated. As of 7- 2013, Activision's CEO raised his salary by more than 600%, while the stock lost its value in double digits.

- Value stocks. Need to know why they become value stocks (i.e. few investors want to own) even they are financially sound. For example, if it is a chip supplier for Apple, there are two primary reasons for its downfall: 1. Apple is declining in sales and 2. Apple is switching suppliers to replace their chip. Technology companies are building better mouse traps. They could turn around in a year or so with better products.

Conclusion

Buying a stock is an educated guess that its stock price will rise. My conclusion is that fundamentals do not always work but they work most of the time:

1. When we buy a value stock, we're swimming against the tide. Hence, we need to wait longer (usually more than 6 months) for the market to realize its value. The exception is the Early Recovery phase (see the Market Cycle chapter) and it has faster and larger returns from most value stocks.

2. Many metrics are intangible and some are misleading. Book value could be misleading for an established company such as IBM. The image of the cowboy in a tobacco company could be a very important asset that is not included in its financial statement.

3. The market is not always rational.

Afterthoughts

- Brand names of big companies are one of the most important intangibles. Here is a strategy to buy big companies in a down market. It has been proven that it works. However, do not just buy these companies without analysis.
  http://seekingalpha.com/article/1324041-buying-brand-names-in-a-bear-market-can-make-you-rich

- The reputation of a company takes a long time to build but a bad incidence to destroy in the case of GM such as the delay in recalling the killer switches.

8   Qualitative analysis

This is the last analysis to evaluate a stock fundamentally. Then the next is technical analysis which is used to find an entry point (also the exit point) for the stock.

Where quantitative analysis fails and why

I find that some stocks with high scores fail and some stocks with low scores succeed as indicated by my performance monitor. The scoring system still works statistically for the majority of my stocks.

- Reasons why stocks with low scores perform in addition to the described in the last discussion:

  o Over-sold. The institutional investors (fund managers and pension managers...) dump them first, and then followed by the retail investors. The big boys will buy these stocks back when they reach a certain price range. RSI(14), a technical indicator described in the Technical Analysis article, is useful to detect these over-sold stocks. This metric is readily available from many sites including Finviz.

  o The falling price improves all fundamental metrics that have the stock price such as P/E and P/Sales.

  o The company has turned around after fixing its problems and/or the market has changed for the better.

  o The current problems have been resolved but not known to the public. It includes resolving a lawsuit, a new product, a new drug, or a new big order, etc.

  o Heavy purchases by insiders. The company's outlook is not shown in its financial statements. Sometimes the insiders hide them so they can buy more of their companies' stocks for themselves.

- Reasons why stocks with high scores plunge in addition to the described in the previous discussion:

- o The company's fundamentals and its prices have reached or closed to the maximum heights. They have no way to go but down. It is particularly true when the stock's timing rating is at or close to the highest point. TTWO that I gifted to my grandchildren had been 5 times doubled in the last few years before it plunged in 2018.

- o It has reached its potential value (or a target price) and it is time to take profits.

- o Sector (or stock) rotation, particularly by institutional investors who drive the market.

- o The outlook of the company, its sector and/or the market is deteriorating.

- o The stock price may be manipulated. There are many reasons to pump and dump the stock. Shorting is not recommended for most investors. However, some experienced shorters make money consistently when they find valid reasons to short the stock.

- o When a new serious lawsuit is pending, a new competing product or drug, canceling a major order, etc.

- o Downgrade by analysts. They could spot some bad events such as product defects, violations of regulations or accounting errors / frauds. The downgrades are more important than the upgrades.

- o The financial statement had been manipulated. The SEC may ask for an investigation.

- o Does not meet the consensus in earnings announcements. Many times investors just over-react.

Qualitative Analysis

We need to do further analysis after the quantity analysis and the analysis on intangibles. Check out the company's prospects. There are sources:

1. Seeking Alpha.

Type the symbol of the company to read as many articles on the company as you have time for. Check out the date of the article and any potential hidden agenda items from the author. Older articles may not have much value. If you cannot find too many good articles, check out the articles from Finviz.com on specific stocks.

Recently, I read an article on AMD and it said it may have good profits in the next two years with the game consoles. The outlook of a company is not shown by any fundamental metric which appears to be a mess. Following a well-known writer, I bought IBM without doing my due diligence (my fault). It went down more than 15% quickly. You can learn from my mistakes.

Be careful on 'pump-and-dump' manipulation written by authors with a hidden agenda. It has happened especially on small companies before even SeekingAlpha.com has less than its share. Here is an article that tells you to sell NHTC. There is an article to tell you to buy ARTX and it most likely is 'pump-and dump'.

2. Research reports. Most likely you can find many free reports from your broker. If you do not, open an account with one that provides such reports. Some subscription services such as Value Line provides such reports.

3. Yahoo!Finance board. Most comments are garbage. However, once in a while you find some great insights. Many times you cannot find any info from other sources on tiny companies elsewhere.

4. The most recent company's financial statements. They are usually available in the company's web site.

5. 10-Ks from Edgar database (www.sec.gov/edgar). Check out new products and its potential competition, key customers, order backlog, research and development and pending lawsuits.

6. Check out the outlook of the sector and the company.

7. Check out its competitors.

8. Some companies are run by stupid people. I received information via my email saying that my mutual fund account could be treated as an abandoned property. I have been cashing dividend checks every year and why it would be considered as an abandoned property. I called them right away to close my account.

The tall and handsome guy presented articulately how he would turn around JC Penny on TV. I could tell you right away that all his tricks had been tried by other companies such as Sears and most did not work. The intelligent investor does not care how handsome, articulated, how rich his family is and how many advanced degrees from prestigious colleges he possesses. If he does not make sense, do not buy his preaching and his company's stock.

It is for the same reason that you read this book. I should read my book repeatedly as I forget what I wrote. If I cannot help you to make money, throw it away and it is a small sum to pay for my book. You should look for your own results, not my good writing.

9. Check out its business model. Some business models do not make business sense. Here are some samples.

- Giving razors makes sense, as the customers have to buy the blades eventually and keep on buying blades for life.
- Supermarket M lowers prices on common merchandises such as Coke and it works. They make money by providing inferior products that you cannot compare prices easily such as meat and seafood. It costs me more time to shop in more than one supermarket.
Eventually there will be a supermarket in my area to satisfy me both in price and quality or at least make a good tradeoff. My time is more important than the savings. They are still making good money.
- Last week it had been brutally hot. I went to a Barns & Noble's bookstore to enjoy reading the updated books and enjoyed the air conditioning. When there are more free loaders like me than customers, the business model does not work.
- Market dumping works to capture the market. Microsoft used to do it with their new Office and Mail products that could not

compete with the established products at the time. Google is following the same model to dump its equivalent products to compete with Office. Now, Microsoft is taking a dose of the same medicine. As of 2015, Google is not winning. Amazon.com gives writers (like myself) great deals if you only sell your digital books via them. This model will work so far as to capture the market today.

Technical analysis (a.k.a. charting) is briefly described here. If the stock is overbought (such as RSI(14) > 60), do not buy a lot as a correction could be possible soon. If the stock is oversold (such as RSI(14) < 25), either the market is wrong or your evaluation is wrong. Be cautious and check again. If there is a breakout (the price rising above the resistance line in the chart), you may want to buy it right away as there is a good chance it may not return to the current price.

Fillers:

My doctor asked me to try an experimental drug to cure my psoriasis. The drug is so strong that it would kill me. However, in either case, my psoriasis will be cured.

The incredible wedding banquet

How to have a wedding banquet that the entire town will talk about and at the least cost? It is in Burger King where they treat you like a king. All the fries are super-sized and the drinks are bottomless. The king's crown, the most popular party favor, is included. Of course, my daughter flatly refused.

9   Research stocks by Technical Analysis

When the stock, the sector that the stock is in and the market both are above its SMA-n averages (Single Moving Average for n days), it is a buy.

1. Bring up Finviz.com from your browser.

2. Enter SPY. Write down the SMA-200 (Single Moving Average for 200 days). Positive numbers indicate the trend for the market is good.

    However, the market could be peaking or overbought. Do not buy stocks when SMA-200 is over 5% and / or RSI(14) is over 65%. RSI is a metric in the same screen.

3. Enter the sector ETF the stock is in. Write down the SMA-50. Positive numbers indicate trend for the sector is good.

    However, the sector could be peaking or overbought. Do not buy stocks when SMA-200 is over 10% and / or RSI(14) is over 65%. RSI is a metric in the same screen.

4. Enter the stock symbol. If your average holding period of the stocks is 50, use SMA-50 and so on. I recommend SMA-200 for holding stocks long term. Write down the SMA-n for your stock. Positive numbers indicate the trend is good.

    However, the market could be peaking or overbought. Do not buy stocks when SMA-200 is over 25% and / or RSI(14) is over 70%. RSI is a metric in the same screen.

If the above three criteria and the fundamental criteria are satisfied, most likely it is a good buy.

Be aware that this discipline requires you spending a lot of time on the screen. That's the reason you do not want to keep more than 15 stocks for this style of investing.

I use technical analysis sparingly on stocks due to my lack of time but I usually marry it with fundamentals.

I use technical analysis more frequently to detect market crashes and sectors that proves to be a better indicator than stocks. Technical indicators usually work better in shorter durations.

My additions to conventional swing trading

Hopefully my additions improve the performance of a strategy that already works.

- I add market timing to Swing Trading. You need to sell most stocks during a market plunge (of course better selling at the peak) and buy them back when the chart indicates so.

- Diversify your portfolio. Keep less than 15 stocks for a portfolio less than a million. Ensure not more than 3 stocks in the same sector. Keep 20 stocks for portfolio over a million. Too many stocks would require more of your time that would be better spent in evaluating stocks. Too few stocks would impact your portfolio when one stock has a big loss.

- Stick with stocks over $2, average daily volume over 8,000 shares (or 6,000 shares for price over $20) and market cap over 200 million in the major three exchanges.

  Most big winners usually are in the price range between $2 and $12 price, and market cap between 200 million to 800 million. These stocks are ignored by the institution investors due to their restrictions. There are exceptions. Adjust the criteria according to your requirements.

- Ignore the subscription services claiming making more than 30% profit consistently. Some even have examples of making 5,000%. Most likely they tell you the winners but not their losers. When they back test their strategies, they cheat their performances with survivorship bias (i.e. those bankrupt stocks are not in the historical database). If their returns are that great, do you think they will share their secrets with you?

10   Order prices

Market orders

Use market orders only when it is necessary (more later) as stocks price can easily be manipulated especially on stocks with low trading volumes.

However, in a rising market, many fast rising stocks can only be bought via market orders. Many winners never take a breather on their way up.

In my momentum portfolio on 11/2013, I placed a sell price for GERN far higher than the market price. Surprisingly I sold it for this price making an annualized return of 1,176% for holding it for 21 days. When there are few or no other sellers for the stock, the market price would be the price you set. If I cannot sell it in the next 9 days (30 days is my holding period for momentum stocks), I would set it lower. Update: One year later, GERN lost 29%.

Sensible discounts

I prefer to buy the stock at the price closest to the last trade price (to most it is the market price). I seldom lose buying these orders. Sometimes I use the day's lowest price to buy (or the highest to sell) plus a penny (or minus a penny for sell prices to sell).

My other purchase strategy is using 0.15% or 0.25% less than the current prices for stocks I really want. For some promising stocks, I buy them at almost the market price and then place another order on the same stock at 0.5% less than the last traded price (and sometimes 2% depending on the current market trend).

We all want to buy less and sell at higher prices. However, if the trade price is too far away from the current market price (such as 5% from the market price), these trades may never be executed. I have had a long list of buy orders that were not executed and turned out to be big gainers. Learn from my bad experiences.

Use a good discount (such as 10% from the market price) if you believe the market, the sector or the stock will dip by 10%. After you bought the stock, you place a sell order 10% more than the price you paid for it hoping the stock will return to the original price and you pocket 10%. Wishful thinking! However, it has happened to me several times primarily due to temporary market dips.

It works when there is a correction and/or the stock is very volatile. It is usually within the 5% range to take advantage of these situations, not the 10% as described. For a 10% plunge, it usually is due to some serious problem of the company surfacing. One common reason is not meeting its earnings expectation and in this case it usually continues its downward trend.

Larger discounts on a falling market

During a falling market (or a mild correction), 3% less than the current prices for buy orders may be fine for some stocks (use 5% for volatile stocks). To illustrate, I placed about 10 of these orders over the last two months during a market dip. Most of the orders were filled. When the market is plunging, do not buy any stock.

Caterpillar and Cisco were some of my buys at these discounts. They were in my watch list to buy. Initially these shares often fall even lower as the trend was downward. As of 12/18/12, CAT earned me from 3% and 14% (bought in 6/12 and 7/12) and CSCO bought in 7/14/12 returned about 34%. My original objective: Buy deeply-valued stocks, wait and sell them when the economy returns.

When you predict the market will dip by 5%, set your buy orders accordingly. Again, predictions are just educated guesses. From my experience, they work most of the time but not all of the time.

On the day of the earnings announcement, the fluctuation of the stock is usually high. Check any change in the earnings estimate before the announcement and act accordingly. Zacks is supposed to be a useful tool to predict earnings estimates. Do not leave orders during the earnings announcement dates, which can be found in Finviz. When the earning turns out to be good, the stock price surges and your order will not be executed. When the earnings are bad, the stock price will plunge usually and you most likely over-payed.

Option expiration dates usually cause more volatility. Retail investors do not have to be concerned except you may use wider stops. In theory, dividend days have little effect on the stock price as it will be lowered by the dividend amount.

High volume of a stock could mean opportunity

High volume usually increases the stock price volatility. If the volatility of a stock increases substantially (such as doubling its average daily volume), there could be important news on the company, recommendation changes from a major analyst or trading by the institutional investors. It usually takes the institutional investors a week to trade a stock with their sizable positions.

Many times it is started by the insiders who know about the breaking news of a stock before it is publicized. Some investment services / sites specialize in identifying the increasing volumes on these stocks.

Because day traders do not want to leave any open positions overnight, higher volatility occurs at the end of the day. It is the same on the day (usually on Friday) when the options are expiring.

Monitor your trade prices

You cannot tell whether you are paying a fair price without keeping a record. To illustrate, you're paying 1% less than the market prices in buying stocks. You may have missed buying some winners. If the 1% you saved is smaller than the appreciation of the stocks you would have bought at market prices, then you should adjust the buy prices to 0.5% less than the market price and monitor again.

Market trend makes a difference too. When the market is trending up, buying any stock would most likely be profitable and usually the purchase orders with higher discounts will not be executed.

Follow the same logic on sell orders. Need to have at least 25 stock purchases (and potential purchases) to make the conclusion meaningful. If you do not trade a lot, you will not have enough data to verify. As described, I prefer not to place an order during the earnings announcement dates which can be found in Finviz.com. If you cannot buy the stock, consider to use market order the next day.

Good prospects

When you find gems especially those stocks that are followed by analysts, buy them at market prices and consider doubling the bet if you are really sure you have a winner. From my super stock screens, I spotted NHTC. I placed several bets and one market order. All of them were NOT executed except with the market order. At the end of the day NHTC is up 18% and my executed order is up 14%. I did not have the best buy but made a good profit. NHTC was on its way to a huge appreciation and I sold it too early. I have earned not to sell a winner and protect the profit with a stop.

Lower the buy for risky stocks (if the beta from Finviz is greater than 1 for example) even if they have good fundamentals.

Quality over quantity

If your time is limited, spend all the time on researching one stock one at a time. However, you need to own at least 3 stocks (more stocks for a large portfolio) for your diversification purposes.

Double your normal purchase position on stocks that look great after the research. For risky stocks that look good, you may want to halve your normal purchase position to cut down on the risk. If you are less risk tolerant, do not buy risky stocks at all. My results are not conclusive on risky stocks but I do get a good sleep.

A recent example

Recently I sold EA with $1 more than my order price but $2 less than the current price of the day, which was the earnings announcement day. I do recommend not placing orders right before the earnings announcement day for the stock. If the earnings are good, you do not get all the profit as in this real example; my broker did get me $1 more. If the earnings are bad, you will not sell it any way. It is the same for buying stocks.

11 When to sell a stock

When the market is plunging or the sector the stock belongs to is deteriorating, sell the stock(s). The other reasons are:

Personal

1. Has met the targets/objectives.
    It could be 10% gain in a very short-term swing, x% return in 4 months for a short-term swing or y% after a year for a long-term trade. Define x and y depending on your risk tolerance and how often you trade.

    I bought 4 stocks in one day during the August, 2015 correction and placed sell orders with 10% more than my purchase prices. I sold one in a day and another one within a month.

    Never look back and do not blame yourself when the prices are better than your trade prices. Adjust your x% and y% to the market. When the market is volatile, use a higher percent. Be disciplined. Stay on the same strategy and detach yourself from emotions.

2. Realize that we have made a mistake. Do not let our ego blocking our eyes. It could be due to bad analysis, unexpected frauds, lawsuits, and/or bad data. It is better to get out with a small loss. I prefer 25% loss as a threshold. A trader may prefer 10% or even less.

    We have to ensure whether it is a mistake or not. If the 'mistake' is just bad luck or due to conditions we cannot possibly predict or control, then it is not a mistake. If it is a mistake, learn from it. When we diversify, one bad loss would not cause a big dent to our portfolios. Stop loss is a good tool most of the time.

    If the criteria have been faithfully followed and it does not work well, check out whether your criteria are wrong or it does not work on the current market conditions.

3. When we have too many stocks in the same sector, we want to replace some to diversify our portfolios.

When the sector is rising, we want to weigh more on the sector at the expense of diversification, and vice versa. Set a limit of how many sectors you are holding.

4. Need cash for living expenses.

5. To reduce tax burden by selling some losers. Tax consideration should not be the primary reason for selling. Take advantage of the difference in long term and short term capital gain treatment.

6. To take advantage of low tax. In 2013, we can pay virtually zero (except the increase of tax on social security payment) Federal income tax on long-term capital gains when our income is below a specific tax bracket (15% as of 2015). Check the current tax laws. Evaluate the sold winners for possible buy back.

Market Timing

7. Follow the market direction, which could be more important than the sector, and in turn which could be more important than the fundamentals of the company.

   For temporary peaks, do not sell all stocks, but those stocks whose fundamentals have been deteriorated more than the other stocks in your portfolio. The objective is to raise cash for buying opportunity.

Deteriorating potential appreciation

8. There may be some stocks that have better appreciation potential than the ones you currently own. Churning the portfolio by replacing better stocks may cost some brokerage commissions and taxes, but it improves the quality and potential appreciation of the entire portfolio.

9. The company's fundamentals have changed for the worse. If you use a scoring system, compare the current score with the score you bought the stock. Apple is a good example from 2013 to 2015. Buy when the fundamentals are good and sell when it is not.

The common ones are expected P/E, the earnings growth rate and the sales growth rate.

When they have passed the peak and started to decline, sell them.

Hints that the fundamentals are degrading

Every bought stock should be evaluated at least every 6 months and its daily news checked (easily done using Seeking Alpha's portfolio function).

- The cash flow is decreasing fast. Cash flow is not a particularly good predicative indicator for appreciation, but a good indicator on whether the company will survive. This metric is very hard to be manipulated.

- A new or pending lawsuit. Check how serious is the lawsuit as companies sue each other all the time.

- When the SEC pays attention to a company, it usually means bad news.

- Increasing receivable and/or inventory.

- Big drop in sales. Do not be alarmed if a new product or a new drug is going to replace a major product. Compare sales to same quarter of prior year to avoid seasonal fluctuations (easily done using Finviz.com).

- Short percentage is increasing fast – someone found something wrong with the company.

- The invalidity of 'one-time charges'.

- Abnormal return rate of the company's pension fund comparing to the average of the companies in the same sector.

- The extravagant life style of the CEO and the many easy loans to officers.

- Too many and too costly reconstructing charges.

- Earnings have been restated too many times.

- Deceptive accounting practice has been discovered.

- A successful product from the competitor or the current product is losing its market share or becoming a low-profit commodity.

- Insiders and/or institutional investors are dumping the companies' stocks far more than the averages especially in heavy volumes.

  o Have more than one insider dumping a lot of the stock within a month and no insider purchase in that month.

  o Have more than one insider decrease their holdings by more than 10%.

- The entire stock market is plunging as indicated by our chart in detecting market crash.
- The stock price does not move up with good news. It shows the price has peaked.
- The accumulation amount is far less than the sold amount. When the stock price is up, the accumulation is less than the sold stocks when the stock price was down last time. It indicates no more accumulation ahead and hence the stock will be down most likely.
- Management deteriorates. One hint is the deteriorating ROE from last quarter.
- Poor operations. They include recalls of products such as the GM recall on ignition switches, product secrets being stolen and customers' credit card info being stolen.

Selling a winner
Even with the above, you may still hesitate to sell a winning horse. It is human nature. Set a stop loss (say 10% below the current price) mentally. You want to do it mentally as you want to avoid flash crash or events you do not have control of such as 911. You do not want to sell your stocks in such events. Adjust the stop loss price when the stock price rises. You will benefit for rising stocks by not existing prematurely. In another words, let the winners rise.

12   Avoid bankrupting companies

Avoid the bankrupting companies at all costs. Here are some hints that a company is going bankrupt:

- I had several companies that had lost most of their stock values. It turns out that most were Chinese companies. I did have some losers from Mexico, Israel and Ireland. I believe most were set up to cheat investors. Most if not all had 'rosy' financial statements. Avoid them, especially small companies in emerging countries.

- Many U.S. companies failed due to fraud, poor management, and/or the management betting wrongly. When the CEO is using the company as his own AMT, or having an extravagant life style, watch out. If they promise you a return doubling the current rate of return of the market, listen to your wise mother: there is no free lunch. Despite so many real examples, still fools are born every day, because greed is a human nature.

- Do not follow the 'commentators' on TV. They have their own hidden agenda which usually is not in your interest.

- Many companies fail due to their lack of ability to pay back their loans. Except for specific industries and situations, avoid companies with high debt (Debt/Equity over 50%). Financial institutions and companies that have high debt in order to finance their products for their customers such as utilities are the exceptions.

- I have a screen named Big Losers beating the market by more than 600% in Early Recovery (a phase defined by me). However, some bankrupted companies are not included in the database which is termed as survivor bias. Hence, the actual result is far worse than the 600%. I still use this screen but skip these companies using the following yardsticks.
    - o The companies are usually safe with high Free Cash Flow / Equity and high Expected Profit / Stock Price.
    - o The following are red flags: low Free Cash Flow / Equity, high Inventory and high Receivable (esp. relative to its Payable), high P/B (over 30) and high net Debt/Equity (over 1 to 3 depending on the industry).
    - o P/PFC should be greater than 0 and less than 50. A healthy cash flow may not be able to service the debt if it is too huge. Hence, compare it to Debt/Equity. Compare the cash flow per year to debt obligations per year.

- New government regulations could bankrupt an industry. What would happen when the U.S. takes out the rebates and subsidies of solar panels? When the U.S. banned solar panels from China, one of my Chinese stocks went bankrupt. Also government bailed out bankrupting companies such as Chrysler (that I made a good profit) and AIG Fannie Mae in 2008.
- Serious lawsuits- Most U.S. companies are required to file this information in their financial reports.
- Obsolete products. Newspapers, retail and similar products would be replaced by the internet. The opposite is new products such as virtual reality products.
- Many companies run out of money during the development phase of the major products. Many are too optimistic in their business plans.
- If you expect the market will recover in 2 years, ensure the company's cash and net income can support their burn rate for at least two more years.
- Many investing sites (most require subscriptions) have safety scores.
- If the Beneish M-Score is greater than -2.22, the company is likely an accounting manipulator.
- Choose companies with Z-Score higher than 3; it does not applicable to financial companies. Both M-Score and Z-Score are available from GuruFocus, a paid subscription. Z-Score does not work for financial institutions.
- Z-Score metrics are: "Working Capital / Total Assets" (A), "Retained Earnings / Total Assets" (B), "Earnings Before Interest & Taxes / Total Assets" (C), "Market Cap / Total Liabilities" (D) and "Sales / Total Assets" (E).
Z-Score = 1.2 A + 1.4 B + 3.3 C +.6 D + E
- Market timing- It does not always work, but it is far better to follow a proven technique than not. It is far safer to take money out of the market when the market is too risky or is plunging. The big losers are companies that provide non-essential products in a down turn.
- Small companies could be risky but very profitable. Typically they have a low stock price (less than $5), small market cap (less than 50 M), low sales (less than $25 M) and low institutional ownership (less than 5%).
- Avoid companies when their own bond ratings are not equal to AAA or AA (www.moodys.com). Section III: Strategies

Section III: Strategies

1   The best strategy

This is the strategy I use every week when the market is not plunging or peaking.

Based on my investment with many subscription services (with a total cost of less than $1,000 per year), I do not have to use the free screening method described. When you have the size of my portfolio, it would be "pound stupid and penny smart" not to subscribe these investment services.

It would not be appropriate to recommend any subscription services here. When they are in business for over 5 years, most likely they are fine. However, they may not perform well recently due to their methods may not be suitable to the current market conditions.

Most offer a month free trial. Set up the screeners as described for all 3 strategies or just the one you will use most. Test out their performance as the durations described. Vary the parameters. Compare the returns to SPY, an ETF simulating the S&P 500 index.

If they have a historical database, a month should be enough. Without a historical database, you have to wait longer to calculate the performances and your test is limited. Hopefully you can test the screens in both a rising market and a falling market.

For this strategy, I use the timing grades. Most subscriptions provide several grades: composite grade, fundamental grade and timing grade (which could be termed as momentum grade).

Compare the grades from several subscription services. If all point out to be positive for a stock, most likely it will be fine. You may want to have a grade yourself composing all these timing grades from subscriptions.
Strategy #2.

This strategy is in the middle ground of the three strategies. It uses fundamentals more than strategy #1.

It is the strategy I use for sector rotation as my annuity provides sector funds that can be rotated every two months without penalty.

Strategy #3.

Among the 3, this strategy has higher chance to keep the stock for a year to qualify for the favorable treatment of long term capital gain.

After three months of holding, check whether it is still worth to hold. If so, hold it for another three months, and so on.

When it suffers a loss and the holding period is less than 365, sell it to qualify for short-term capital loss. If not, wait for one more day, sell covered call to generate some income. Check the current tax law on capital gains.

2   Tom's conservative strategy

The following is a summary of Tom's conservative strategy as described in his profile in Seeking Alpha web site. Use it as an example and modify it to fit your investing philosophy. You need to ignore your friends telling you how much money he is making when the market is up. You also need not to tell them how much money you're not losing otherwise you do not have any friend.

I believe the best performance is achieved matching a strategy to the current market conditions and there is no Holy Grail in investing.

Click here for Tom's strategy.
(http://tonyp4idea.blogspot.com/2012/05/tom-armisteads-investment-strategy.html)

A winning strategy for couch potatoes

My friend Tom (no relationship) has a very similar strategy similar to Tom's. My friend is making money with the least risk. He only buys stocks after the market crashes and sell stocks when the market rises. Ignore all market pundits. It is recommended to anyone who does not have time to monitor his/her investment.

Enhance a good strategy.
Following the favorable stages to trade in the market cycle described in this book, buy in the Early Recovery phase (about 1 ½ year after the crash or use the entry point described in the chapters on Market Timing), sell in one or two years after and maintain cash for the rest of the time.

Optionally add a small amount of purchases in Nov. 1 and sell them in April 1. Optionally buy in Dec. 1 and sell in Feb. 1 to take advantage of the best (statistically) period of the year. Add long term bonds when the interest rate is high (say more than 5%) and you do not have to sell these bonds.

Spend the rest of the time in the comfortable couch (i.e. enjoying life) or sip some fancy tropical drink served by some beautiful tropical lady in some nice tropical island. Not a bad strategy!

Top down approach

1. Is it a good time to buy stocks (via market timing)?
2. What sectors to buy?
3. Screen out about 10 stocks in that sector.
4. Further evaluate each stock.
5. Optionally, use Technical Analysis to see the best time and price to buy the selected stocks.
6. Periodically monitor your stocks. Sell some if necessary and go to Step 1.
7. When you buy at the bottom, buy value stocks only.

The easiest retirement planning system

Have a budget and live within your means. Buy good stuffs that last for a long time. After saving enough cash for emergency and planned expenses such as vacation, new car, college, etc., invest your extra money in a retirement account (Roth IRA if allowable) with 80% in a market ETF and 20% in a short-term bond ETF.

Run the chart described in the market cycle chapters once a month. If the chart tells you to exit the market, move all to cash. Reenter the market when the chart tells you so. It beats most if not all of your financial plans from the best experts money can buy.

Afterthoughts

My late friend had a 'buy and hold strategy' that worked pretty well. Most of his stocks were big companies. He died with a house worth more than a million and many millions in stocks. His only mistake was not to transfer more of his stocks to his heirs before his death. He died on the year when the estate exemption returned back to a million. Uncle Sam was the biggest winner and won big without any effort.

3   Screen the Insiders' purchase.

Bring up OpenInsider.com
(http://www.openinsider.com/)

Tuesday, Nov 19, 2013 2:39pm EST

OPENINSIDER .COM

SEC Form 4 Insider Trading Stock Screener

Enter Symbol Search

Real-time insider transaction data, 5 min auto-refresh

SEC Form 4 Screener

Home | Latest | Top | By Sector | By Symbol | Charts | Contact

Insider Transactions

Filing Date	All dates
Trade Date	All dates
Symbol	Symbol or CIK
Insider	Name or CIK

☑ Officer
☐ CEO
☐ CFO
☐ Director
☐ 10% Owner
☐ Other

SIC Industry	Min Max
Transaction	All Codes
Share Price $	Min Max
Trade Value $	Min Max

Sort by Filing Date

☐ Max Results
☐ Exclude derivative-related

Submit Clear

Latest Insider Purchases $25k+

SEC Form 4	Trade Date	Sym	Company	Insider	Relationship	Shares	Transaction	Value
Nov 19 02:32pm	Nov 18 2013	OCN	Ocwen Financial Corp	Hayes Timothy M	EVP, Gen Counsel, Secretary	1,000	Purchase at $52.44	$52,440
Nov 19 02:14pm	Nov 18 2013	ONTX	Onconova Therapeutics, Inc.	Reddy E Premkumar	Director	5,000	Purchase at $12.10	$60,500
Nov 19 01:37pm	Nov 18 2013	MVIS	MicroVision Inc	Tokman Alexander Y	President, CEO	20,000	Purchase at $1.35	$27,000
Nov 19 01:26pm	Nov 18 2013	CEN	Center Coast Mlp & Infrastructure Fund	Curran Michael F	Director	5,000	Purchase at $19.00	$95,000
Nov 19 01:15am	Nov 15 2013	PDII	Pdi Inc	Belle Gerald P.	Director	20,400	Purchase at $5.21	$106,286
Nov 19 12:54pm	Nov 15 2013	MCBF	Monarch Community Bancorp Inc	Ross Stephen Milerd	Director	12,500	Purchase at $2.00	$25,000
Nov 19 12:47pm	Nov 15 2013	MCBF	Monarch Community Bancorp Inc	Mitchell Martin L	Director	100,000	Purchase at $2.00	$200,000
Nov 19 12:35pm	Nov 15 2013	MCBF	Monarch Community Bancorp Inc	Loomis Karl F	Director	125,000	Purchase at $2.00	$250,000
Nov 19 12:11pm	Nov 19 2013	MM	Millennial Media Inc.	Palmieri Paul J.	President, CEO	10,000	Purchase at $5.92	$59,220
Nov 19 11:42am	Nov 15 2013	AF	Astoria Financial Corp	Chrin John R	Director	1,668	Purchase at $22.17	$36,758

Source: OpenInsider

The following is for illustration only. This screen is displayed on 11/19/2013.

If your e-reader's screen is too small, bring up your PC's browser, and type: http://ebmyth.blogspot.com/2013/12/insider-screen-for-profit-from-insider.html

Here is an illustration looking for candidates.

- Select Officer only. Director is fine too.
- Ignore the transactions that have values less than $100,000. We only have PDII and MCBF. You should not have the same stocks on a different date. Select the stocks that have purchase values more than $100,000.
- Next bring up Finviz.com in your browser. Enter PDII and scroll on the way down to find the net purchase (= purchase amount – sold amount). For example, if the insiders bought $100,000 worth of stock and they sold $100,000 of your stock, it would not be considered as a purchase. There was no insider sell for PDII, so it is fine.
- Was the stock bought close to the market price? From Finviz.com again, the purchase price was $5.25 and the current price is $5.29. So it looks good.

Summary of selected criteria

The displayed screen does not have all the selection criteria and sorting order as below.

- Select Officer only.
- Filing Date and Trade Date within the last 7 days.
- Transactions: Purchase only.
- Sorted by Value. Omit transactions less than $100,000 (adjust to the value you're comfortable with).

Skip the stocks if they are of the following (change them to your own requirements).

- The purchase price is not close to the market price.
- Penny stocks (less than $2) or market cap less than 50 million. It is your call.

- Stock daily volume less than 8,000 shares (I prefer 10,000).
- Poor fundamentals. If you do not have time to do a thorough analysis, use Blue Chip Growth's grade. GuruFocus.com (fee) has a nice evaluation with warning signs.
- If they are not listed in one of the three major exchanges.

My steps

Be flexible and use the tools you have.

1. Select the stocks with heavy insider trading. Use OpenInsider.com. Select Officers, Purchase Only, and Last 7 Trade Days and Last 7 File Days. Sorted by Trade Value.

2. Use Finviz.com. Understand the company and their fundamentals.

   If the stock cannot be found, most likely it is not traded here. Skip these companies and the companies with small market caps and average daily volumes.

   Check the insider trade prices. If the trade prices are too low from the market prices, skip these stocks.

   Understand the company such as the country, the sector and general financial shape. I would skip most foreign countries especially from emerging countries and small companies that I do not trust their financial information.

   For safety, I would examine the stocks further when they are losing money.

   Skip the companies that have more than 5% appreciation in the last 5 days. We may have missed this boat but there are many other boats.

3. Use OpenInsider.com again to list the 90 days transactions (all) for the stock. If the CEO sells 1,000 shares and buys back 1,000 shares, there is no insider purchase.

4   A turnaround strategy for value stocks

Many value stocks tend to stay in this phase for a long time. When the turnaround starts, it could be very profitable.

Market Timing

Do not buy any stock when the market is risky as described elsewhere in the book. Actually you should sell most of the stocks when the market is risky.

Buy Metrics

Metric	Value	Conservative	Aggressive
General			
Market Cap	>300 M	>1,000 M	>100 M
Price	> 2	>10	>1
Avg. Volume	>20,000	>50,000	>10,000
USA	Only	Only	Foreign but listed in USA
Fundamental			
Forward P/E	<15	<10	<25
Earning Gr Q-Q	>5%	>8%	>3%
ROE	>10	>15	>5
P / FCF	<10	<8	<15
Debt / Equity	<.5	<.25	<1
Technical			
SMA-50%	>10	>15	>5
Misc.			
Blue Chip Growth	A or B	A	A or B
Fidelity	>6	>8	>5
IBD	>60	>90	>50
Vector Vest	>=1	>=0.8	>=12
Value Line Proj. 3-5% return	>5%	>10%	>5%

Zacks	>=4	5	>=4
ASSS	>=2	>=5	>=2

The assignment values for the metrics are not fixed; feel free to change it according to your own risk level. I do have suggestions for conservative investors and aggressive investors.

Some of the metrics are not readily available in Finviz.com and the following describes how to modify them.

Explanation

- Market Cap. The free version of Finviz.com does not allow you to specify the range. Use 'Any' and then select the stocks according to the specified values. Average Volume has the similar restriction.

- The conservative values for Market Cap, Price and Average Volume try to select larger companies. The aggressive values try to select smaller companies, which historically are more risky but perform better.

- I prefer 'USA' for Country. Stay away from small companies from developing countries unless you can trust their financial statements.

- Forward P/E measures the value of the stock. Ensure "E" (Earnings) is positive. I prefer it over P/E (from the last twelve months).

- Earnings Growth Quarter to last Quarter is preferred to be positive unless it is during a recession.

- ROE measures how well the company has been managed.

- P/FCF. "Price / Free Cash Flow" cannot be manipulated easily. Together with low "Debt / Equity", it measures whether the company would bankrupt.

- SMA-50%. Some stocks tend to stay in a value stage for a long while (termed value trap). We like to select stocks just starting being noticed and on its way up.

- Misc. Many sites have evaluated the stocks for us. Some only let their customers to access such information, some are available for free trials or are available from the library.

- ASSS is my scoring system.

With the above, I have 35 stocks on 10/28/16. If you need 10 stocks for further evaluation, try to sort Forward P/E in descending order and select the top 10. If you cannot find any or substantially less than normal, it implies the market is risky, so take a break. If the performances of the last few stocks you selected are poor, take a break too as the market conditions do not favor the value metrics we specified.

Qualitative analysis

Double click on the stock and read as many articles described on the stock as possible. If it meets all the criteria, buy the stock. Recommend to use market orders for large companies in a non-volatile market (when the average daily fluctuation is less than 0.5%). If the selected stock is the one you just sold, make you only buy it after 31 days to avoid Wash Sale penalty.

Keeping informed

Check the company updates of the stock you owned every month. One easy way is to enter the stocks in a portfolio in SeekingAlpha.com.

Sell the stock

Re-evaluate the stocks every 6 months.

If it does not meet the criteria or the market is risky, sell it. If it is only a few days away from the long-term capital gain, sell the losers right away or hold on the winner for a few more days.

Re-balance the portfolio after a stock has been sold. Ensure it is diversified enough into large/small cap and sectors.

Top-down Investing

It is similar to the above. Find the sectors that perform the best last month. Under Finviz.com, select the best sector under 'sector' one at a time. Several sites such as Fidelity compare the stock to the averages of stocks in the same sector.

Section IV: Advanced Topics

1   The power of market timing

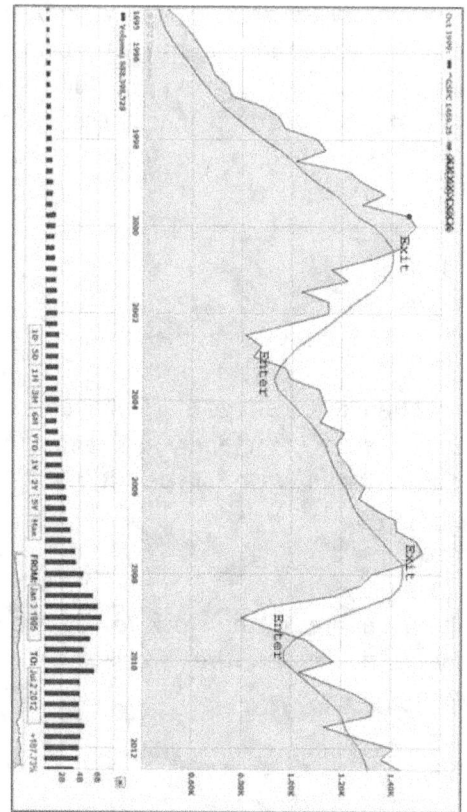

Most e-book readers allow you to select the graph to make it fit entirely to your screen. Detecting market plunges indicates the exit points and reentry points from 2000 to 9-2009 as follows.

Table: Vital Dates

Market Plunge	Peak	Bottom	Indicator Exit	Indicator Reenter
2000	08/28/00	09/20/02	10/01/00	06/01/03
2007	10/12/07	03/06/09	02/01/08	09/01/09
			08/01/11	11/01/11

As of 04/2014, my chart (from Yahoo!Finance) still indicates to invest fully in the market. For simplicity I skip a few brief exits and reentries since 2011. Run the simple chart once a month. When it indicates a potential market plunge is closer, run the chart once a week.

It is based on stock prices so it may not identify the peaks and bottoms precisely, but so far it has never failed to avoid big losses and ensure big gains by reentering the market. Hope it will give us enough time to act in the next market plunge as the last two did.

Unbelievable return with market timing

Calculate how much you made if you followed the above exit points and reenter points from 2000 to today. I bet you would make a good fortune.

To test the effect of market timing, I calculated the return of S&P 500 with market timing and compare it to the return of S&P 500 without market timing from 1-2000 to 9-2013.

There are many assumptions to make the calculations easier. In general, dividends are not considered. Compounding is not considered in most cases. The return with market timing should be substantially better if we buy a contra ETF during exits and sell it during reentries.

I was shocked by the incredible return by using simple market timing and the chart tells us to exit and reenter the market only 3 times from 2000 to 2013.

Summary info:

S&P 500 1-2000 to 9-2013	With Market Timing	Without Market Timing
Better	**500%**	
Gain	1,000	167
Gain %	68%	11%
Annualized gained	5%	1%
Days	4,959	4,959

Calculations:

S & P 500	With Market Timing	Without Market Timing
1-2000	1,469[1]	1,469[1]
Exit 10/01/00	1,041[2]	1,041
Enter 06/01/03	1,041	964[4]
Exit 02/01/08	1,489[3]	1,379[4]
Enter 09/01/09	1489	1,020[5]

Exit 08/01/11	1,888	1,293
Enter 11/01/11	1,888	1,251
09/03/13	2,469	1.638
Gained	2,469 – 1,469=1,000	1,638-1,469=167
Gain %	1000/1469 = 68%	167/1469 = 11%
Annualized gained	68% * 365/4959=5%	11%*365/4959=1%
Better	(1,000-167)/167 = 500%	

Portfolio with Market Timing:

[1] Both start with S&P 500 of 1,469 on 1-3-2000.
[2] 10/01/00
The market timing portfolio exits the market and remains same value of 1,041 until 6/1/00.
[3] 02/01/08
The market timing portfolio exits the market and remains same value of 1,489 until 9/1/09.

'1,489' is calculated as follows:
1,041 * (1 + Rate) = 1,041 * (1 + 1,379-964)/964) = 1,489
where S&P 500 is 964 on 6/1/00 and 1,379 on 2/1/08.

The other calculations are based on S&P 500 is 1,020 on 9/1/9, 1,293 on 8/1/11, 1,251 on 11/1/11 and 1,636 on 9/3/13.

Portfolio without Market Timing:

[1] Both starts with S&P 500 of 1,469 on 1-3-2000. We could use the the S&P 500 value on 9/3/13, but it will not account on some compounded interest consideration.

[4] S&P 500 is 964 in 6/1/00 and 1,379 on 2/1/08.

[5] 02/01/08. The portfolio value is calculated to be 1,020 as follows:
1,379 * (1 + Rate) = 1,379 * (1 + (1020-1379)/1379) = 1,020
where S&P 500 is 1,379 on 2/1/08 and 1,020 on 9/1/09.

The other calculations are based on S&P 500 is 1,293 on 8/1/11, 1,251 on 11/1/11 and 1,636 on 9/3/13.

I cannot believe the shocking return with market timing. I checked my calculation and there was nothing wrong but do not hold me on this. Ignoring the compound rate of return should be minor. If you have time, send me your e-mail address to pow_tony@yahoo.com, so I can send you the spreadsheet to check out any error.

Even if I made a mistake somehow and got 100% instead of 500%, it still doubles the return without market timing! Ask any fund manager what it means to his or her fund performance and his / her career.

It will detect the next market plunges, but it may not give us ample of time to react as the last two did. It will not detect the precise bottoms and peaks as they depend on the stock price of an ETF representing the market. I have separate statistics on market peaks and bottoms but they have not been proven. The above may not work as effectively if there are too many followers. On the contrary it may work as it could be a self-fulfilling prophesy.

The stock prices of SPY are obtained from Yahoo!Finance. The entry and exit points are obtained from my simple chart from Yahoo!Finance described and they are subject to my interpretation.

2   Market timing by calendar

The following predictions are based on historical data. You may have slightly different findings depending on when you start and when you end your testing.

You can load the historical data of SPY via Yahoo!Finance and check out how close you are or different from my own predictions. They are my predictions based on historical data. Use it as a reference only.

- Presidential cycle.
  Usually the market performs worse in the first two years after the election than the next two. During the 3rd year the president has to make the economy look rosy in order to buy votes. Statistically it is the best year for the market and is followed by a good year (the election year). The government may stimulate the economy, the stock market and employment by printing more money, lowering interest rates and lowering taxes.

Democratic presidents have better market performance statistically than Republican presidents. This is not too logical as though Republicans are more pro-business traditionally.

- Olympics.
It has been proven that the host country has a better chance that its stock market appreciates the year after the Olympics. It could be due to the exposure from the Olympics and / or the huge expenses in preparing for the Olympics.

The last two Olympics follow this pattern as of 12/23/2013:

Olympics Country / Year	ETF	Period	Return
United Kingdom / 2012	EWU	Jan. 3, 2013 - Dec. 23,2013	11%
China / 2008	FXI	Jan. 3, 2009 - Dec. 31, 2009	43%

Greece could be an exception. It is too small a country to host this world-class event and it has wasted too many resources by building too many white elephants that the country can never justify. Brazil depends on its export of natural resources to China, so I do not count on the Olympics effect there.

Winning a lot of Olympic medals has no prediction for the stock markets. Both the Russian Empire and E. Germany were winners but disappeared in their original forms afterwards.

- Seasonal.
Best profitable investment period is: Nov. 1 to April 30 of the following year. It is similar to the saying 'Sell in May and Go away'. It did not work since 2009 as it was an Early Recovery (defined by me) in the market cycle.

The market does not always happen as predicted. However, when more folks follow this, it becomes a self-fulfilling prophecy. I prefer "Sell on April 15 and come back on Oct. 15" to act before the herd. The more practical strategy is to start selling in April 1 and become more aggressive (selling at closer to the market prices) when it is close to May 1. For the last five years, I did not find this prediction reliable.

The explanation of the 'summer doldrums' could be that the investors cash their stocks for vacations and college tuition in the fall. Buying quality companies at the dips could be profitable.

- The worst month: September.
  The next worst month is October. However, if there is no serious market crash during October (and this month has more than its shares of crashes), it could be the best month to buy stocks.

- The best month for the bull: November.
  However, several market bottoms occurred in October and November. The next strong month is December.

- Best 30 days: Dec. 15 to Jan. 15, next year.
  It was correct for the period of 2012-2013.

- Window dressing.
  Institutional investors sell their losers and buy winners around Nov. 1. From my rough estimate and on the average, the winners have a 2% percentage point gain better than the market and the losers have 1% worse than the market.

  I recommend that you evaluate the top 10 winners from the last 10 months or YTD in Oct. 15 and sell them at 3% gain or two months later.

  I recommend that you buy in Dec. and sell them 3 months later. Include the stocks with more than 30% loss for the last 11 months or YTD, sort them by Earning Yield in descending order and evaluate the top 10 stocks.

  In both cases, do not buy foreign stocks and stocks with return of capital. Ignore stocks not in the three major exchanges, with low volumes and stock prices less than $2. Do not buy in losing years such as 2007 and 2008. I have my tests with my own assumptions and I use tools not available to most readers.

This is a guideline only. Do not buy any stocks during market plunges. Current events should be considered first such as a potential war and the hiking of interest rates.

Epilogue

Thanks for reading. If you find this book useful, please write a brief, unbiased review. When you have mastered the techniques in this book, read Appendix 2 for my book Complete the Art of Investing and the Kindle version has over 850 pages (6*9), about 3 times the average book on investing. As of 02/2018, I do not know any of my reviewers and all profits so far have been donated to charities. Unless otherwise stated, most fillers if not all are original and created by me.

Appendix 1 – All my books

- Complete the Art of Investing (highly recommended combining most of my books on investing). The Kindle version has over 850 pages (6*9), about 3 times the size of an investing book.
- Sector Rotation: 21 Strategies and another book Shorting (highly recommended for short-term investors) have more specific chapters on the topic and share many articles with "Complete the art of investing".
- Best stocks for 2022 (avail after Dec. 15, 2021).
- "Nuclear War with China".
- Books for today's market: Profit from Coming Market Crash.
- The following books are in a series: Finding Profitable Stocks, Market Timing and Scoring Stocks. Alternate books: Using Fidelity and Using Finviz.
- Books on strategies: "Profit from bull, bear and sideways markets" (Rotation + Momentum + ETF Rotation + trend following), Trading System (similar to printed version of Complete), Swing (Rotation + Momentum), ETF Rotation for Couch Potatoes, Momentum, SuperStocks, Dividend, Penny & Micro Stock, and Retiree.
- Books for advance beginners: Be an expert (highly recommended), Introduce, Investing for Beginners, Beat Fund Managers, Profit via ETFs, Buffett, Ideas, Conservative and Top-Down.
- Miscellaneous: Lessons in Investing. Investing Strategies. Buy Low and Sell High. Buy High and sell Higher. Buffettology. Technical Analysis. Trading Stocks.
- Concise Editions and Introduction Editions are available at very low prices and are competitive with books of similar sizes (50 pages) and prices ($3 range).

Most books have paperbacks. Links and offers are subject to change without notice.

Best stocks to buy for 2022 (avail. after Dec. 15, 21)

We care about performance only. Not considering dividends and fees, my last three books in this series have beaten the SPY (the market to most) by **110%, 71% and 25%** from the publish date to 07/01/2021.

Book	Stocks	Return	Ann.	Beat SPY by
Best Book for 2021 2nd Edition	10	20%	52%	110%
Best Book for 2021	4	29%	52%	71%
Best Book to Buy from Aug, 2020	14	42%	45%	25%
Avg.	9	31%	50%	69%

Appendix 2 – Complete the Art of Investing

Instead of buying 16 books, why not buy one book (Complete the Art of Investing) consisting of 16 books? Besides saving money and your digital shelve space, it gives you quick reference and concentration on the topic you're currently interested in. It covers most investing topics in investing excluding speculative investing such as currency trading and day trading.

The Kindle version has about 850 pages (6*9), about the size of three books of average size. With the cost of $10 and at least 850 investing ideas, it is about one cent per idea. Most other books have only a few ideas in the entire book

The 16 books

This book "Complete Art of Investing" is divided into 16 books as follows. Click for the link to the book described in Amazon.com. I squeezed more than 3,000 pages into 850 pages by eliminating duplicated information such as evaluating stocks.

Book No.	Amazon.com
1	Simple techniques
2	Finding Stocks
3	Evaluating Stocks
4	Scoring Stocks
5	Trading Stocks

6	Market Timing
7	Strategies
8	Sector Rotation
9	Insider Trading
10	Penny Stocks & Micro Cap
11	Momentum Investing
12	Dividend Investing
13	Technical Analysis
14	Investing Ideas
15	The Economy
16	Buffettology

The book links are subject to change without notice.

"How to be a billionaire" is for beginners and couch potatoes, who can use the advanced features of this book in the simplest and less time-consuming techniques. Most advance users can skip this section unless they want to use some of the short cuts described.

We start with the basic books Finding Stocks, Evaluate Stocks, Trading Stocks and Market Timing. You can select and start with one of the many styles and strategies in investing such as swing trading and top-down strategy. Many tools are described in other books such as ETFs, technical analysis, covered calls and trading plan.

Many books start with "Why" to lure you to read more and are followed by "How" and then the theory behind the book.
If the book you're reading is beneficial to you, imagine how it would with 850 pages.

Most readers' comments are on "Debunk the Myths in Investing", which this book is originally based on. As of 2018, I did not know any of the commentators on my books.

"I skipped ahead to his chapter book 14 (of "Complete the Art of Investing"), Investment Advice just to get a feel of his writing style. His research is phenomenal and doesn't overwhelm with big words or catchy "sales-like" tactics.

I truly believe this ordinary man, Mr. Tony Pow, has a gift of explaining his experience as an investor without the bull crap of trying to make you buy his stuff. He seemingly just wants to share his knowledge, tips, and clarity of definitions for the kind of folks like me who want to understand something FIRST before jumping in with emotions of trying to make a boat load of money. I like the technical analysis side he brings.

Mr. Tony Pow talks about hidden gems in his book; well....quite frankly, he is a hidden gem. Thank you and I will also post my comments about this author to my Facebook page!" – JB on this book.

"Excellent book, recommend to all investors... great knowledge. It has fine-tuned my investing strategies... Your book is hard to set aside, as I read it all the time learning good techniques and analysis of stocks, ETF... Since I purchased your book in March, I have underlined, highlighted and placed tabs on top of pages for quick reference." – Aileron on this book.

"Tony, I just finished reading your 2nd edition. It's my pleasure to report that I found it most interesting. You're welcome to use this blurb if you like:

Debunk the Myths in Investing is an all-encompassing look at not only the most salient factors influencing markets and investors, but also a from-the-trenches look at many of the misconceptions and mistakes too many investors make. Reading this book may save not only time and aggravation but money as well!"

Joseph Shaefer, CEO, Stanford Wealth Management LLC.

"Tony, Great work!" from James and Chris, who are portfolio managers.

"'Debunk the Myths in Investing' is a comprehensive book on investing that deals with many aspects of this tense profession in which with a lot of knowledge and a bit of luck (or vice versa) one can greatly benefit...

Therefore 'Debunk the Myths in Investing' is an interesting book that on its 500 pages offer a lot of knowledge related to investing world and many practical advice, so I can recommend its reading if you're interested in this topic."
- Denis Vukosav, Top 500 Reviewers at Amazon.com.

"490 pages (Debunk) of a genius's ranting and hypothesis with various theories throughout, written light-heartedly with ample doses of humor...Yes, the myth of not being able to profitably time the market is BUSTED...

One might ask... Why is he giving away the results of his hard-earned research for only $20? He states that his children are not interested in investing and wants to share his efforts with the world." - Abe Agoda.

"Excellent book, recommend to all investors... great knowledge. It has fine-tuned my investing strategies... Your book is hard to set aside, as I read it all the time learning good techniques and analysis of stocks, ETF... Since I purchased your book in March, I have underlined, highlighted and placed tabs on top of pages for quick reference." - Aileron on this book.

"Great stuff, Tony. It's great to meet experienced traders such as yourself. I had a browse through the book and think your method is a little more refined than mine."
"Your strategy is very rules based and solid. I sometimes envy people who have developed something like this."

Making 50% in one month
I claim to have the best one-month performance ever for recommending 8 or more stocks without using options and leverage. My following return is 57% in a month or 621% annualized. They are slightly different as I calculated the average from the averages of three different accounts. The average buy date is 12/26/18 and the "current date" is 01/28/19.
The performance may not be repeated. I will use the same screen for the coming years and even the expected 10% (or 120% annualized) is very good.

I used the same screen for searching stock candidates. I spent a total of about 20 hours from Dec. 15, 2018 to Jan. 5, 2019.

Stock	Buy Price	Sold or Current Price	Buy date	Sold or Current date	Profit %	Profit % Ann.	Status
CHK	2.13	2.99	01/03/09	01/18/19	40%	982%	Sold
MNK	16.41	21.45	01/03/19	01/25/19	31%	510%	Sold
MNK	16.43	21.45	01/03/19	01/25/19	31%	507%	Sold
NNBR	5.68	8.58	12/26/18	01/28/19	51%	565%	
NNBR	5.72	8.58	12/26/18	01/28/19	66%	727%	
ESTE	4.35	6.45	12/26/18	01/18/19	48%	766%	Sold
LCI	4.61	8.29	12/21/18	01/28/19	80%	767%	
MDR	8.01	9.13	01/08/19	01/28/19	14%	255%	

YRCW	3.29	5.78	12/21/18	01/28/19	76%	727%	
YRCW	3.26	5.78	12/21/18	01/28/19	77%	742%	
ASRT	3.56	4.18	12/26/18	01/28/19	17%	193%	
UTCC	7.13	11.00	12/26/18	01/28/19	54%	600%	
YRCW	2.92	5.78	12/26/18	01/28/19	98%	1083%	

Best one-year return

I claim to have the best-performed article in Seeking Alpha history, an investing site, for recommending 15 or more stocks in one year after the publish date without using options and leverage.

https://seekingalpha.com/article/1095671-amazing-returns-velti-alcatel-lucent-alpha-natural-resources

Your choice

"Complete the art of investing" should be your first choice. If you are short-term trading, I recommend "Sector Rotation: 21 Strategies" and "Shorting Stocks /ETFs". These 3 books together with "Using Fidelity" share many articles.

My recommended stocks can be found in my "Best stocks" series. It would be published on Dec. 15 – it is not a promise. So far, this book and "Sector Rotation: 21 Strategies" are my best sellers. All info are subject to change without notice.

Sector Rotation: 21 Strategies

In addition, as of 5/2020 I bet that no author besides me made **over 4 times** using sector rotation starting the amount more than his yearly salary then.

- On 5/26/2020, I searched for "Sector Rotation" under Amazon's Book. They are listed in the same order except my book Sector Rotation: 21 Strategies.

Book	Date	Size[1]	Kindle $[1]	Hard $
Sector Rotation: 21 Strategies	**05/2020**	**425**	**$9.95**	$24.95
Super Sectors	09/2010	289	$26.39	$49.95
Dual Momentum Investing	11/2014	240	$40.40	$42.20
Sector Investing	05/1996	260		$29.94
Sector Trading Strategies	08/2007	164	$26.39	$16.66
The Sector Strategist	03/2012	225	$26.39	$44.96

ETF Rotation	10/2012	125	**$9.95**	**$14.99**
Optimal... Sector Rotation	07/2015	80		$44.07

[1] From Amazon on size and prices as of 5/25/2020. Last update is 09/2021.

My book won in all categories except the price for hard copy in one. However, my book won as the lowest cost per page by a wide margin.

- I have **21** strategies in sector rotation while most books have only one. It ranges from simple rotation of a stock ETF and cash for beginners to many advanced strategies for experts. Most other books have one or two strategies.
- Andrew, a contributor on Sector Rotation article at Seeking Alpha, said, "Great stuff, Tony. It's great to meet experienced traders such as yourself. I had a browse through the book and think your method is a little more refined than mine."
- "You have written the book in a way that makes good and logical sense." Bill.
- Do not be fooled by past performances. Just check the recent performance of the top 50 stocks selected by IBD in the last five years. The mediocre result (hopefully it will change) could be due to too many followers and/or there is no evergreen strategy.
- I switched most (if not all) of my sector funds in April, 2000 from technology sectors to traditional sectors (better to money market fund). We can reduce losses by spotting market plunges and the sector trend.

Appendix 3 - Our window to the investing world

The paperback version of this chapter can be found in the following link.
http://ebmyth.blogspot.com/2013/11/web-sites.html

- **General**
  Wikipedia / Investopedia /Yahoo!Finance / MarketWatch / Cnnfn / Morningstar /CNBC / Bloomberg / WSJ / Barron's / Motley Fool / TheStreet

- **Evaluate stocks**
  Finviz / SeekingAlpha / MSN Money / Zacks / Daily Finance / ADR / Fidelity / Earnings Impact / OpenInsider / NYSE / NASDAQ / SEC / SEC for 10K and 10Q (quarterly) reports required to file for listed stocks in major exchanges.

- **Charts**
  BigCharts / FreeStockCharts / StockCharts /

- **Screens**
  Yahoo!Finance / Finviz / CNBC / Morningstar /

- **Besides stocks**
  123Jump / Hoover's Online / FINRA Bond Market Data / REIT / Commodity Futures / Option Industry

- **Vendors**
  AAII / Zacks / IBD / GuruFocus / VectorVest / Fidelity / Interactive Brokers / Merrill Lynch /

- **Economy.**
  Econday / EcoconStats / Federal Reserve / Economist /

- **Misc.**
  Dow Jones Indices / Russell / Wilshire / IRS / Wikinvest / ETF Database / ETF Trends / Nolo (estate planning) / AARP /

Appendix 4 - ETFs / Mutual Funds

What is an ETF

ETFs have basic differences from mutual funds: 1. Lower management expenses, 2. Trade ETFs same as stocks, and 3. Usually more diversified but not more selective than the related mutual funds such as NOBL vs FRDPX.

The major classifications of ETFs are 1. Simulating an index such as SPY, QQQ and DIA, 2. Simulating a sector such as XLE and SOXX, 3. Simulating an asset class such as GLD and SLV, 4. Simulating a country or a group of countries such as EWC and FXI, 5. Managed by a manager(s) such as ARKK, 6. Betting a market or sector to go down such as SH and PSQ, and 7. Leveraged (not recommended for beginners).

Fidelity: Index ETFs (https://www.fidelity.com/etfs/overview).

Wikipedia on ETF (http://en.wikipedia.org/wiki/Exchange-traded_fund).

List of ETFs
ETF database (Recommended): http://etfdb.com/
ETF Bloomberg: http://www.bloomberg.com/markets/etfs/
ETF Trends: http://www.etftrends.com/
A list of ETFs. Seeking Alpha.
http://etf.stock-encyclopedia.com/category/)
A list of contra ETFs (or bear ETFs)
http://www.tradermike.net/inverse-short-etfs-bearish-etf-funds/
Misc.: ETFGuide, ETFReplay
Fidelity low-cost index funds:
https://www.youtube.com/watch?v=zpKi4_IJvlY
Fidelity Annuity funds with performance data.
http://fundresearch.fidelity.com/annuities/category-performance-annual-total-returns-quarterly/FPRAI?refann=005

Other resources
Most subscription services offer research on ETFs. IBD has a strategy dedicated to ETFs and so does AAII to name a couple.

Seeking Alpha has extensive resources for ETF including an ETF screener and investing ideas. So is ETFdb.

Not all ETFs are created equal
Check their performances and their expenses.

When to use or not to use ETFs
I prefer sector mutual funds in some industries, as they have many bad stocks such as drug industry, banks, miners and insurers. Most mutual funds cannot time the market.

When you believe a sector is heading up (or contra ETF for heading down), but you do not have time to do research on specific stocks, buy an ETF for the sector; it is same for the market.

Half ETF
Taking out half of the stocks that score below the average in an index ETF could beat the same full ETF itself. I call it HETF (half the ETF). You heard it here first. To illustrate, sort the expected P/E (not including stocks with negative earnings) in ascending order and only include the stocks on the first half. Add more fundamental metrics. It will take a few minutes.

Disadvantages of ETFs
- When you have two stocks in a sector ETF one good one and one bad one, the ETF treats them the same. Stock pickers would buy the one that has a better appreciation potential.
- Sometimes the return could be misleading due to stock rotation. To illustrate this, on August 29, 2012, SHLD was replaced by LYB in a sector fund. SHLD was down by 4% and LYB was up by 4% primarily due to the switch. Unless you sell and buy at the right time (which is impossible), your return would not match the ETF's returns due to the replacement.
- Ensure the performance matches the corresponding index; it is hard due to excluding dividends.

Advantages of ETFs
- We have demonstrated that you can beat the market by using market timing. Between 2000 and Nov., 2013, you only exit and reenter the market 3 times and the result is astonishing.
- It is easy to rotate a sector vs. buying/selling all of the stocks in this sector. Rotating a sector is the same as trading a stock.

- The risk is spread out, and your portfolio is diversified especially for a market ETF or buying three or more ETFs in different sectors.
- Periodically the bad stocks in most funds are replaced by better stocks.
- Eliminate the time in researching stocks.

Leveraged ETFs

I do not recommend them. Some are 2x, 3x and even higher. They're too risky for beginners. However, when you are very sure or your tested strategy has very low drawdown, you may want to use them to improve performance. Most leveraged ETFs and contra ETFs have higher fees.

My basic ETF tables

I include some contra ETFs, mutual funds and Fidelity's annuity. Some of these may be interesting to you.

ETFs and funds come and go. Some ideas and classifications are my own interpretation. Refer to ETFdb for updated information. Not responsible for any error. Check out the ETF or fund before you take any action.

Table by market cap:

Category	ETF	Mutual Funds	Fidelity's Annuity	Contra ETF	Alternate
Size:					
Large Cap	DIA	See Blend		DOG	
	SPY			SH	FXAIX VOO
	QQQ			PSQ	FNCMX
	RYH				
Blend	IWD	BEQGX			
Growth	SPYG	FBGRX			FSPGX
Value	SPYV	DOGGX			FLCOX
Dividend	NOBL	FRDPX			
	VYM				
Mid Cap			FNBSC	MYY	
Blend	MDY	VSEQX			
Growth		STDIX			
		BPTRX			
Value		FSMVX			

			FPRGC	SBB	FSSNX
Small Cap					
Blend	IWM	HDPSX			
Growth		PRDSX			FECGX
Value		SKSEX			FISVX
Micro	IWC				
Multi					
Blend		VDEOX			
Growth		VHCOX			
Value		TCLCX			
Total					FSKAX
Bond					
Long Term (20)	VLV	BTTTX		TBF	
Mid Term (7 – 10)	VCIT	FSTGX			
Short Term (1 – 3 yrs.)	VCSH	THOPX			
Total	BOND	PONDX			
Corp Invest Grade	VCIT	NTHEX			
High Yield (junk)	PHB	SPHIX			
Muni	MUB	Check state			
Special situation					
Buy back	PKW				

Table by sectors:

Sector	ETF	Mutual Funds	Fidelity's Annuity
Banking[1]		FSRBK	
Regional	IAT		
Bio Tech	IBB	FBIOX	
	XBI	Large	
Consumer Dis.	XLY	FSCPX	FVHAC
Consumer Staple	XLP	FDFAX	FCSAC
Finance	KIE	FIDSX	FONNC
	IYF		
Energy	XLE	FSENX	FJLLC

Energy Service		FSESX	
Gold	GLD	FSAGX	
Gold Miner	GDX	VGPMX	
Health Care	IYH	FSPHX	FPDRC
	VHT	VGHCX	
House Builder	ITB	FSHOX	
	ITB	Perform	
Industrial	IYJ	FCYIX	FBALC
Material	VAW	FSDPX	
	IYM		
Oil	USO		
Oil Service	OIH	FSESX	
Oil Exploration	XOP		
Real Estate	VNQ	FRIFX	FFWLC
REIT	VNQ		
Retail	RTH	FSRPX	
	XRT		
Regional bank	KRE	FSRBX	
Semi Conduct	SMH		
Software	XSW	FSCSX	
	IGV		
Technology	XLK	FSPTX	FYENC
	FDN	FBSOX	
		ROGSX	
Telecomm.	VOX	FSTCX	FVTAC
Transport	XTN		
	IYT		
Utilities	XLU	FSUTX	FKMSC
Wireless		FWRLX	

Footnote. [1] Also check Finance.

Table by countries outside the USA:

Country	ETF	Mutual Funds	Fidelity's Annuity	Alternate
Australia	EWA			
Brazil	EWZ			
Canada	EWC	FICDX		
China	FXI	FHKCX		
EAFE	EFA			
Emerging	VWO	FEMEX	FEMAC	FPADX
Europe	VGK	FIEUX		
Global	KXI	PGVFX		
Greece	GREK			
India	INDY	MINDX		
Indonesia	EIDO			
Latin America	ILF	FLATX		
Nordic		FNORX		
Hong Kong	EWH			
Japan	EWJ	FJPNX		
S. Africa	EZA			
S. Korea	EWY	MAKOX		
Singapore	EWS			
Taiwan	EWT			
	TUR			
United Kingdom	EWU			
Foreign:				
Combination				
Intern. Div.	IDV			FTIHX
Small Cap	SCZ			
Value	EFV			
Europe	VGK			

#Filler: Honey, my book can play music.

https://www.youtube.com/watch?v=HxGT5z6d-GA&list=PLMZa6mP7jZ2b1otqG4tfbgZpLEdh6YiNF

It may cut down commercials by casting it to TV.